VMware View Security Essentials

The insiders guide on how to secure your VMware View Environment

Daniel Langenhan

BIRMINGHAM - MUMBAI

VMware View Security Essentials

First published: July 2013

Production Reference: 1190713

Published by Packt Publishing Ltd.
Livery Place
35 Livery Street
Birmingham B3 2PB, UK.

ISBN 978-1-78217-008-2

www.packtpub.com

Cover Image by Jarek Blaminsky (milak6@wp.pl)

Credits

Author
Daniel Langenhan

Reviewers
Christian Rudolph
Ramses Smeyers

Acquisition Editor
Andrew Duckworth

Commissioning Editor
Mohammed Fahad

Technical Editors
Sharvari H Baet
Jalasha D'costa
Pratik More
Amit Ramadas

Project Coordinator
Amigya Khurrana

Proofreader
Amy Guest

Indexer
Monica Ajmera Mehta

Graphics
Abhinash Sahu
Ronak Dhruv

Production Coordinator
Nilesh R. Mohite

Cover Work
Nilesh R. Mohite

About the Author

Daniel Langenhan is a client-focused virtualization expert with more than 18 years of international industry experience.

His skills span the breadth of virtualization, ranging from Architecture, Design, and implementation for large multitier enterprise client systems to delivering captivating education and training sessions in security technologies, and practices to diverse audiences.

He also possesses an extensive knowledge and experience in Process management, Enterprise level storage, and Linux and Solaris operating systems.

Utilizing his extensive knowledge, experience, and skills, he has a proven track record of successful integration of virtualization into different business areas, while minimizing cost and maximizing reliability and effectiveness of the solution for his clients.

He has gained some experience working with major Australian and International vendors and clients. Daniel's consulting company is well established with strong industry ties in many verticals; for example, Finance, Telecommunications, and Print. His consulting business also provided services to VMware International.

I would like to thank my wife Renata for her tireless support, without her this book would have not been possible.

About the Reviewers

Christian Rudolph is a Cloud consultant who has worked with virtualization technologies since 2003. He started as a virtualization infrastructure architect and worked in several server consolidation projects. Later, he built the operational team for the virtualization and was the responsible technical lead for this. During this time, he also got in touch with possible virtualization solution for end users, where he was part of some projects to build virtual desktops for end users. Since 2012, he is responsible to build and design the cloud solution of his company with a focus on infrastructure-as-a-service and desktop-as-a-service.

Christian holds the VCP-DCV 2/3/4/5 certification and has been also selected as a vExpert in 2013.

Ramses Smeyers is part of Cisco Technical Services where he works with the Datacenter Solutions support team. His main job consists of supporting customers to implement and manage Cisco UCS, VDI, and VXI infrastructures. He has a very strong background in computing, networking, and storage, and has more than 10 years of experience deploying enterprise and service provider datacenter solutions. His relevant certifications include VMware VCP/VCAP DCA|DCD/VCDX, Cisco CCIE Voice, RHCE, and Cisco Data Center Unified Computing Support Specialist.

www.PacktPub.com

Support files, eBooks, discount offers and more

You might want to visit www.PacktPub.com for support files and downloads related to your book.

Did you know that Packt offers eBook versions of every book published, with PDF and ePub files available? You can upgrade to the eBook version at www.PacktPub.com and as a print book customer, you are entitled to a discount on the eBook copy. Get in touch with us at service@packtpub.com for more details.

At www.PacktPub.com, you can also read a collection of free technical articles, sign up for a range of free newsletters and receive exclusive discounts and offers on Packt books and eBooks.

http://PacktLib.PacktPub.com

Do you need instant solutions to your IT questions? PacktLib is Packt's online digital book library. Here, you can access, read and search across Packt's entire library of books.

Why Subscribe?

- Fully searchable across every book published by Packt
- Copy and paste, print and bookmark content
- On demand and accessible via web browser

Free Access for Packt account holders

If you have an account with Packt at www.PacktPub.com, you can use this to access PacktLib today and view nine entirely free books. Simply use your login credentials for immediate access.

Instant Updates on New Packt Books

Get notified! Find out when new books are published by following @PacktEnterprise on Twitter, or the *Packt Enterprise* Facebook page.

Table of Contents

Preface

Most people associate security with network security and focus on firewalls and network monitoring. But security is more than that. It starts with establishing a stable environment, protecting this environment not only from intrusion but also from malicious intent. Last but not the least it is about tracking the issue and recovering from it. All this is security and needs to be addressed.

What this book covers

Chapter 1, Introduction to View, gives a short overview of what a typical View environment contains as well as definitions of all the technical terms we will be using.

Chapter 2, Securing Your Base, explains that a VMware virtual machine image is hardware independent, replacing the physical corporate desktops with thin clients makes changes to the corporate desktop image a lot easier as well as centralizing the management of it. This centralization also creates the need to rethink provisioning and redundancy compared to the traditional IT methods. As everyone who uses a vDesktop is now dependent on the centralized virtual environment, it is of the upmost importance that this infrastructure is safe and available. We will discuss how to harden the View servers and integrate them into the existing VMware vSphere settings, such as HA, DRS, and event monitoring. We will also take a bit of time to understand how View logfiles work and how to read them.

Chapter 3, Securing the Connection, explains that corporate working environments are not limited to one site and it becomes more and more important for personnel to work from other places than the office. In being able to operate in the new mobile world it is even more important to secure your environment against intrusion. This chapter focuses on network security like firewalls, DMZ deployments, and user authentication.

Chapter 4, Securing the Client, addresses the issue of securing the client which most corporations find critical. Most corporate data theft comes from within the organization not from external threats and data theft. This means not only the control of who is able to log into what is of importance, but also addressing the usage of USB devices that can be used to extract corporate data.

Chapter 5, Backup and Recovery, deals with fundamental things that most people don't associate with security, but which still is of the upmost importance. Backup and restore of the VMware View environment itself is explained in this chapter.

What you need for this book

In this book we are focusing on VMware View 5.1 based on a VMware vSphere 5.1 environment. A typical View environment consists of:

- VMware ESXi 5.1 server
- VMware vCenter 5.1 (including SSO and all other requirements)
- Shared storage
- VMware View 5.1
- Windows desktop images

In regards of the ESXi servers, as of writing of this book there are two versions of ESXi 5.1: the standard one (Build 799733) and the View 5.1 compatibility version (VMware-VMvisor-Installer-201210001-838463.x86_64.iso). Only the View 5.1 supported ESXi 5.1 version should be used, see also VMware KB 2035268.

I also assume that you have a working knowledge of VMware View and are able to do the following tasks:

- Installing VMware View Servers
- Deploying a Windows 7 Workstation template in View
- Deploy desktop pools
- Access vDesktops via the View Client and HTTP interface

Later we will make use of additional View Connection Servers, View Transfer Servers, and View Security Servers. As I like to show you in this book how to configure and secure View, as space is limited, you will need to familiarize yourself with how to install the basic features. We will however discuss all the details of the security design and how to configure the components.

In addition to all this you need to have either physical or virtual network infrastructure. In *Chapter 3, Securing the Connection*, we will play with the network features. For this you need to be able to configure a firewall (blocking ports, enabling NAT, and Port forwarding), and create an isolated network. If you don't have the hardware for this I would suggest having a look at VMware vShield.

Who this book is for

This book is written for the novice as well as for the professional. As a novice, you should have some experience with View, at least you should have it installed once. As a professional it will give you a deeper understanding on how the different View components play together to generate security.

Conventions

In this book, you will find a number of styles of text that distinguish between different kinds of information. Here are some examples of these styles, and an explanation of their meaning.

Code words in text are shown as follows: "The URL contains the HTTPS protocol as well as port 443."

New terms and **important words** are shown in bold. Words that you see on the screen, in menus or dialog boxes for example, appear in the text like this: "Navigate to **View Configuration | Servers**."

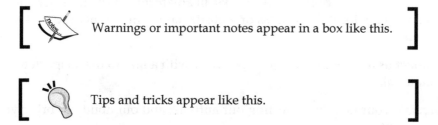

> Warnings or important notes appear in a box like this.

> Tips and tricks appear like this.

Reader feedback

Feedback from our readers is always welcome. Let us know what you think about this book—what you liked or may have disliked. Reader feedback is important for us to develop titles that you really get the most out of.

To send us general feedback, simply send an e-mail to feedback@packtpub.com, and mention the book title via the subject of your message.

If there is a topic that you have expertise in and you are interested in either writing or contributing to a book, see our author guide on www.packtpub.com/authors.

Customer support

Now that you are the proud owner of a Packt book, we have a number of things to help you to get the most from your purchase.

Errata

Although we have taken every care to ensure the accuracy of our content, mistakes do happen. If you find a mistake in one of our books—maybe a mistake in the text or the code—we would be grateful if you would report this to us. By doing so, you can save other readers from frustration and help us improve subsequent versions of this book. If you find any errata, please report them by visiting http://www.packtpub.com/submit-errata, selecting your book, clicking on the **errata submission form** link, and entering the details of your errata. Once your errata are verified, your submission will be accepted and the errata will be uploaded on our website, or added to any list of existing errata, under the Errata section of that title. Any existing errata can be viewed by selecting your title from http://www.packtpub.com/support.

Piracy

Piracy of copyright material on the Internet is an ongoing problem across all media. At Packt, we take the protection of our copyright and licenses very seriously. If you come across any illegal copies of our works, in any form, on the Internet, please provide us with the location address or website name immediately so that we can pursue a remedy.

Please contact us at copyright@packtpub.com with a link to the suspected pirated material.

We appreciate your help in protecting our authors, and our ability to bring you valuable content.

Questions

You can contact us at questions@packtpub.com if you are having a problem with any aspect of the book, and we will do our best to address it.

1
Introduction to View

Virtual Desktop Infrastructure (VDI) not only opens the door to easy desktop virtualization, but it also opens possibilities of security breaches.

We live in a world where security is paramount. As our daily life becomes more and more online-based, we need to understand more about how to secure our life online. The trend toward replacing existing physical desktops with VDI is rapidly strengthening, especially with the strong emergence of tablets and other high-end mobile devices coupled with wider and faster mobile network access. It is not only accessibility that drives the process, corporations are driven by the rising cost of CBD floor space, investment reductions in physical desktops, and the ability to centralize user data and management are key motivators for adoption of VDI. Corporations are reducing the amount of office space by introducing working-from-home schemes, using hot desks and providing the ability to work from anywhere, anytime. VDI makes this possible, thus enabling users to take their desktop home, or to the coffee shop around the corner. However, this introduces new risks to the corporate desktop environment that were not apparent before.

Corporations now have to deal with:

- Network security for remote users
- The ability of users to access confidential corporate information offsite
- Securing data against theft using a simple USB stick
- Redirecting printing to the nearest printer

VMware View is one of the leading VDI products. Its strength is that it builds upon existing capabilities, features, and investments made into the VMware infrastructure. This book will focus on the essential security features and how to address them using VMware View. Let's start off with defining what View actually contains.

VMware View definitions

You might be already familiar with most of this; however, I think a quick refresher is not a bad idea. The VMware View product is based on VMware vSphere. Let's just go over the vSphere 5.1 products that are needed to create a vSphere environment.

- **ESXi**: The base workhorse of virtualization. This is where VMs live and run.

- **vCenter**: This manages multiple ESXi servers, is responsible for creating cluster, run HA, DRS, and is responsible for features such as vMotion.

- **Single Sign-On (SSO)**: This is a new addition to vSphere in 5.1 and is responsible for Identity management. However, there is currently no integration for View into SSO.

- **Inventory Service**: This keeps an inventory of vSphere objects, making the response time for inventory requests faster, creating less load onto the vCenter service.

- **WebClient Server**: VMware announces that the WebClient interface will in future replace the Windows-based vSphere Client. The WebClient has some advantages compared to the vSphere Client; however, it requires people to change their thinking as things look and feel differently.

The View environment consists of the following products that may need to be installed:

- **View Connection Server**: This is the main component for View. It contains the HTTPS-based View Administrator interface. The heart of the operation View Connection Server comes in four varieties:

    - **Standard**: The main component. You will need one install of this. We will look at it in this chapter.

    - **Replica**: A replica server is used for load balancing and failover capacity. It is basically an additional Standard Connection Server. We will look at it in this chapter.

    - **Security**: The security server can be deployed in a DMZ and forward incoming View Client connection to a View Standard Server. We will look at this in the *Chapter 2*, *Securing Your Base*.

    - **Transfer**: The transfer server is a buffer service between the View Connection Server and local desktop images (check in and out). We will look at this in the *Chapter 2*, *Securing Your Base*.

- **View Composer**: This is used to reduce the amount of storage used for the virtual desktops by creating View Linked Clones. It also reduces deployment time of desktops as not the full desktop has to be cloned.

- **View Persona Management**: The Persona Manager helps with the synchronization of roaming profiles. It is an extra service that needs to be installed. We will look at this in *Chapter 3*, *Securing the Connection*.

- **View Agent**: This is installed on the virtual desktop that is the source template for a given pool of virtual desktops. It is also responsible for things like USB redirection and Single Sign-On.

- **View Client**: The View Client comes for almost any operating system out there including iPad and Android. It enables the ability to connect to a View Connection Server. It comes in two versions: the normal one and the one that allows to checkout a desktop to a local computer.

- **View desktop**: This is a Virtual Machine (VM) that contains a desktop OS and is provisioned by a View desktop pool.

- **ThinApps**: ThinApps is a product that allows you to virtualize and package an application. We will not be able to discuss this feature in this book due to the page limitation.

Now after this short inventory, the following diagram illustrates how these components work together:

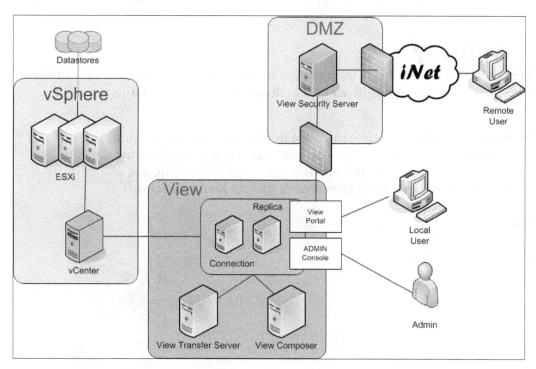

Downloading the color images of this book

We also provide you a PDF file that has color images of the screenshots/diagrams used in this book. The color images will help you better understand the changes in the output.

You can download this file from: `http://www.packtpub.com/sites/default/files/downloads/0082EN_Graphics.pdf`

In addition to this, we have several services that a View installation offers:

- **View Administrative Console**: This is the interface that manages the View environment. It is an HTTPS-based interface that is installed as part of the View Connection Server (Standard).

- **View Portal**: The View Portal is an HTTPS interface that lets people select and connect to a virtual desktop. It is installed as part of the View Connection Server (Standard).

- **View desktop pool**: A View desktop pool is a collection of rules that define how View desktops are deployed.

Summary

This short chapter holds the introduction to this book. It gives an overview of the View infrastructure elements, as well as defining the technical terms we will be using.

In the next chapter, we will start with a quick overview and definition of the View environment, followed by security considerations of the underlying vSphere environment. We will also talk about logging and SSL certificates, and build up a View Replication Server and then shortly discuss load balancing it.

2
Securing Your Base

In this chapter we will take a good look at the base installation of View, its configuration settings, and how to secure the base of your virtual desktop deployment. We will start with a look at the base structure that View builds on — vShpere.

vSphere considerations

Before we start with the View considerations, let's step back a second and understand what basic security concepts have to be implemented on the vSphere level in order to secure the whole virtualization stack that VMware View depends on.

Using View means that you are using vSphere. Desktop virtualization centralizes the desktop infrastructure onto the core virtualization stack. Therefore if the core virtualization (vSphere) is not available, View will not be available; meaning anybody that uses a virtualized desktop will not be able to work. The cost implications are clear.

When we are talking about vSphere security, we have to understand that this encompasses a multitude of topics. As this book is focusing mainly on View, I will only touch this topic briefly.

The vSphere stack is built from a minimum of one VM/appliance, but in most cases we are talking about two to three VMs. Best practices for scaling and security dictate that vSphere uses a dedicated database server. For scaling purposes, it is a very good idea to split the vSphere 5.1 services: **Single Sign-On (SSO)**, **Inventory Service**, **Virtual Center (vCenter)**, and **WebClient** into at least two VMs, one VM that runs SSO and the WebClient and one that runs vCenter and the Infrastructure Client. SSO and WebClient have a one-to-many (1:n) relationship with vCenter, therefore allowing for easy scalability.

In addition to this we need at least one VM for the View Connection Server, but ideally we would want more, as we would want additional View Connection Servers, Security Servers, Composers, and Transfer Servers. This ends up to be quite a lot of VMs. If these VMs fail or are running out of resources, they start impacting the vSphere and View environment. Therefore, considering the vSphere Cluster settings is very important.

A rather important fact to know is that View 5.1 can have a maximum of 32 ESXi hosts per cluster if NFS is used as the filesystem.

VMware High Availability (HA)

When we are talking about vSphere Cluster settings, it is important to understand that we need to separate workloads. Beat practice for VMwares states that all management VMs are protected by **High Availability (HA)** and **Dynamic Resource Scheduling (DRS)** (HA being able to restart failed VMs and DRS responsible to relocate the VMs to load balance the cluster).

All essential vSphere Management and View Management VMs should be located in their own cluster and have the following cluster HA settings:

- **HA VM Restart Priority**: HIGH
- **HA VM Monitoring**: HIGH

DRS should be enabled and automated. I personally use a DRS group that makes sure that all essential vSphere VMs (DB, SSO, and VC) are (a "should" not a "must" rule) kept on the first host in the cluster. This allows me, in a failure situation, to access the essential VMs directly without searching all the hosts for them.

Workload VMs (the Virtual desktop VMs) are best kept on a dedicated cluster. If this is the case, DRS should be switched on for them. Switching on HA will reduce the available resources for the desktops. Activating HA will mean that you will either lose a whole ESXi Server (**n+1** setting), or a given percentage of the total amount available (% settings). If an ESXi Host fails, the View desktop currently deployed on it will also fail. Depending on the type of View desktop pool used, this isn't such a big deal as a user would just reconnect to the portal and choose a new desktop. HA might make sense for persistent desktops that are critical to the business, such as Admin desktops.

So, the choice is basically spending extra money on hardware (for HA redundancy) or accepting limited blackouts.

If they share a cluster with other VMs, it might be a good practice to exclude them from HA (possible with scripting, but rather complicated), or at least reduce the default HA restart priority. The reason behind this is that in case of a host failure, the production VMs should recover first and foremost. In general a production database, e-mail, or CRM system is more important and causes more interruption to the business than a couple of desktops. Worst case, if HA isn't configured correctly, the result could be that the Virtual desktops start up; however, no resources are left to start the production systems.

Fault Tolerance (FT)

FT can be used with View desktops, however I cannot imagine any desktop that would need it. Firstly, FT only supports one vCPU; secondly, costs for an FT desktop with regards to resources used is rather large, increasing the cost (in $) for a given desktop. Any FT-enabled VM requires double the amount of resources (basically one copy of the VM on two different ESXis).

Personally, I find that FT for View Servers doesn't make sense due to the costs involved.

DRS and resource pools

If you have to share a production environment with a View environment, it is good to consider some basic inputs. The VMware recommendation is to separate View and production workload. Please also keep in mind that the licensing agreement doesn't allow you to run non-View VMs on a View-licensed cluster.

As Virtual desktops have, compared to Servers, a smaller CPU and memory footprint, DRS is essential for any View environment. This is especially the case in share environments. Virtual desktop workload in most business cases is more time-dependent then server workload. Virtual desktop workload follows the office hours, meaning that they are most active between 9-12 and 13-18 on workdays. A typical problem with Virtual desktop environments is in the morning. As everyone more or less starts around 9:00 a.m., the demand on the underlying vSphere environment is extremely peaking at this time. This can pose a problem in shared environments when a lot of desktops start consuming memory and CPU at the same time, as the underlying systems are impacted. A design with no resource pools can lead to starved production servers. Situations like these are called Boot Storms; we will look into this a bit more from the client's perspective in *Chapter 4, Securing the Client*.

The best practice in a share environment is to create resource pools for different types of workloads and adjust the memory and CPU shares to suite the importance of the systems. This is mostly done by understanding the money value that these systems represent. For example, the wage of one worker for one hour against the significant business impact of e-mail servers or web servers. In addition to adjusting the shares, it is essential to use reservations and limitations on these resource pools. If there are no resource pools, all VMs share memory and CPU on the same level. In general, we should have a minimum of three resource pools: one for production workload, one for management workload, and one for the View workload. As the management workload is rather important, maybe even as much as the production servers, we should put a reservation on it that supplies it with the absolute minimum CPU and memory for it to function. If the amount of Virtual desktops is known and doesn't change, a limitation on the resource pool should be considered. Last but not least, I would recommend that the shares for the production pools are set to HIGH. However, determining the right setting is not a straightforward task, and requires knowledge of your environment and the business impact of the various workloads.

Resource pools for dedicated View clusters follow a slightly different approach. In a dedicated cluster, the consideration for resource pools is how many different desktop pools are using this cluster. If the cluster is used only for one desktop pool, no resource pool is needed. If there are different types of View desktop pools for different functions and purposes, resource pools can be used to prioritize resource allocation. Following the same logic discussed earlier, we have to determine which pools are more important than the others and then assign resources appropriate for them.

Capacity planning

Capacity planning is one of the most ignored topics. When businesses start virtualization, especially desktop virtualization, people believe that VMs do not cost any money or are freely available. This can lead to immense problems very quickly. As I said before, security is not only about intrusion but also about availability. If your vSphere environment is out of resources, such as CPU, memory, storage, or even network bandwidth, it poses a risk to the whole environment. Businesses that use free resources of their production environment to host virtual desktops will realize huge savings, as free capacity is used and so they save on buying full-desktop computers or dedicated hardware for virtual desktops. However, it also poses the following risk. If not configured correctly, the capacity drain of all the virtual desktops can impact the production servers. Another aspect is to realize how fast virtual desktop environments can grow. It happens quite a lot that Proof-of-Concept environments become productionized, as the need for fast adaption is demanded from management. The next thing that happens is that these environments run out of resources as hardware can't be purchased or added fast enough for the demand.

In order to mitigate this risk capacity, planning should be done. This can either be done using a spreadsheet, or by using VMware Operations Manager for View if the environment is more complex.

Basic View hardening

We now will talk about the steps to harden the View environment.

vSphere hardening

Hardening your vSphere installation is a rather important point; however, it is going beyond the focus of this book. Please have a look at the following official *VMware vSphere 5.1 Hardening Guide*:

```
http://communities.vmware.com/docs/DOC-22981
```

Operating system (OS) hardening

I will just quickly mention that one cannot harden View properly without first hardening the Windows operating system that View resides on. As we want to focus on View hardening, I will just point out the typical OS hardening points as follows:

- Windows Updates
- Password policies
- Antivirus

We will discuss, in the next chapter, Windows Firewall settings. However, Windows hardening that is already in place is mostly sufficient for View.

User accounts

To install and operate View you could use just one user account, the domain-Admin account. However, this would enable an attacker to gain control of the whole system or an unintentional password change of the admin account, which would disable the whole system. The other very good reason to use several user accounts is logging. The best example is the vCenter log; if View uses a dedicated user account log, actions can be very easily identified between normal workload and view workload. The following user accounts should be used:

- **View connection account**: This account connects the View Connection Server to vCenter. The minimum required rights can be found in the *VMware View Installation Guide* on page 87. If the View Composer is installed on the vCenter, this account must be a part of the Windows local administrator group.

- **View Composer account**: If the View Composer is installed standalone, this account is used by View Composer to talk to vCenter, The minimum required rights in vCenter can be found in the View installer Guide on page 88.

  View Composer requires this account also to be able to create and destroy computer accounts in AD. Therefore, the setup of this account is part of the installation routine and described in detail in the *VMware View Installation Guide* on page 27.

- **View Administration Console accounts**: During the installation, you can choose which user group has administrative access to the View Administration Console. It is recommended to create a separate group for this task.

- **View Client group**: Creating one or ore AD groups to manage the View installation is always a good idea. If clients with local mode are used, these should always be in a separate account from View users without local mode.

  Separating View users into multiple groups will enable administrators to track usage and also to control behavior and entitlements of several view groups.

- **Database user accounts**: The View Composer and the View Event database needs user accounts and these should be separate accounts to all the other ones.

A View Administrator Console user

By default, during install you define what user account will be associated with the View Administrator group. Additional users and groups can be assigned to the various View roles. The setting can be accessed via **View Administrator Console | View Configuration | Administrators**. The following screenshot shows the **Global Administrators View** window.

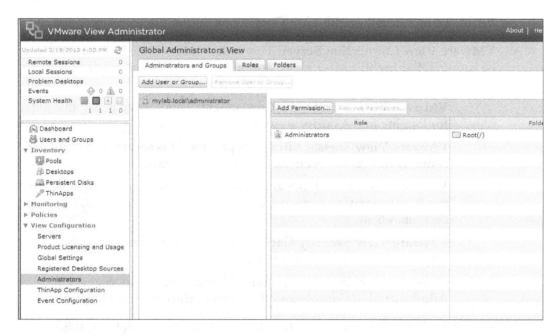

The following roles are available:

- **Administrators**
- **Administrators (Read Only)**
- **Agent Registration Administrators**
- **Global Configuration and Policy Administrator**
- **Global Configuration and Policy Administrator (Read Only)**
- **Inventory Administrator**
- **Inventory Administrator (Read Only)**

In addition to the existing roles, new roles can be configured. It is very important to choose who can access the View Administrator Console, as all security settings can be changed here. The best practice is to create a separate AD group to manage access to the View Administrator Console.

Services

It is rather important to know what services have to be running in the View window's VMs for View to function correctly. System monitoring tools like IBM Tivoli, BMC Patrol, or the free but also powerful Nagios or Cacti can monitor these services and take actions when they fail. These actions are typically a restart of the service and/or trigger an alarm.

The services to be monitored on the View Connection Server are:

- **VMware View Connection Server**: This is the main service that must be running. Staring this service also automatically starts and stops the following services:

    ◦ **VMware View Framework Component**: This service is responsible for logging and security services.

    ◦ **VMware View Message Bus Component**: This service provides the communication between the various View components.

    ◦ **VMware View PCoIP Secure Gateway**: This service is only active if the PCoIP Gateway service is configured (refer to *Chapter 3, Securing the Connection*).

    ◦ **VMware View Security Gateway Component**: This service is responsible for the secure tunnels.

    ◦ **VMware View Web Component**: This service produces the View Administration Console and the web interface for the View portal.

- **VMware View Script Host**: This service is not enabled by default. It is responsible for running third-party scripting.

- **VMware VDMDS**: This service is responsible to provide LDAP services to View. It is essential that this service runs.

The services to be monitored on the View Security Server are basically the same as on the View Connection Server:

- **VMware View Security Server**: The main service that has to be running. This service starts and stops the following services:

    ◦ **VMware View Framework Component**: This service is responsible for logging and security services.

º **VMware View PCoIP Secure Gateway**: This service is only active if the PCoIP Gateway service is configured (refer to *Chapter 3, Securing the Connection*).

º **VMware View Security Gateway Component**: This service is responsible for the secure tunnels.

The services to be monitored on the View Transfer Server are as follows:

- **VMware View Transfer Server**: The main service that has to be running. This service starts and stops the following services:

    º **VMware View Transfer Server Control Service**: This server is for management and for communication with the View Connect Servers.

    º **VMware View Framework Component**: This service is responsible for logging and security services.

- **Apache2.2 service**: This service provides a method to transfer data between View Clients with local modes and the View Transfer service.

Logging

Logging works in the following way.

The Event Database

The **Event Database (DB)** stores all events that occur with a View Connection Server in a SQL DB. This sounds rather weak but actually can be extremely useful. The events stored in the DB can be read out with a business analyzing software such as Crystal Reports, IBM Cognos, and others, which enable the correlation between View and business events. This automatically provides a tool to find out what business event has the View desktop and user triggered. The power this gives for investigation should be clear. Also, it lets you understand who logged on when and where.

We now will configure the Event DB:

1. Create a new Microsoft SQL or Oracle database (refer to *VMware View Installation Guide* for more details).
2. Log in to the **View Administration Console**.

3. Navigate to **View Configuration | Event Configuration**. The following screenshot shows **VMware View Administrator**:

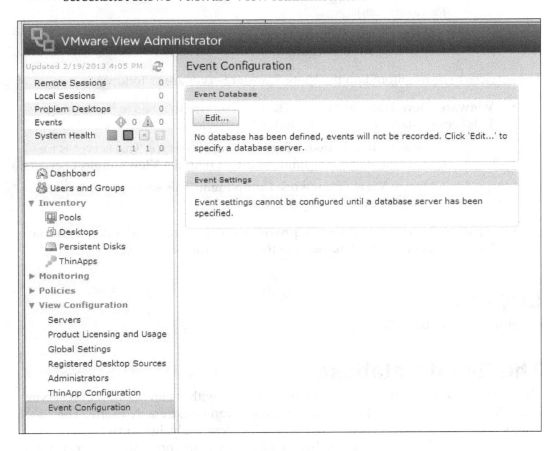

4. Click on **Edit**.

5. In the following menu you now can attach a SQL Database or Oracle Database to View. The table prefix can be used to separate tables if the View Event DB is co-located with other data in the same database. The following screenshot shows **Edit** event database:

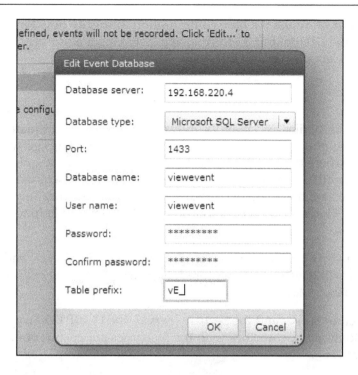

6. After clicking on **OK** the database is attached. The following screenshot shows the **Event Configuration** window:

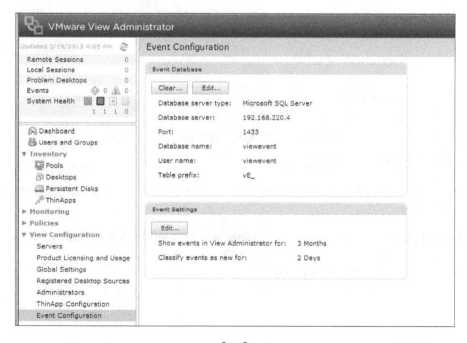

7. You can now adjust the base configuration to specify how long events are kept in the DB (default **3 Months**) and how long a new event should be classified as new (default **2 Days**).

Logfiles

The importance of logfiles and their locations cannot be underestimated. Logfiles should be the first go-to point for any administrator when things go wrong. Understanding where the logfiles are will increase the chances to quickly track down problems with the View system. As we have already discussed if View is down or desktops are not available, productivity is reduced, meaning the business is losing money. The second point is that some of the files will help to track down security breaches.

The logs for the View Connection Server, the View Security Server, and the Transfer Server will have its logfiles stored in `[install Drive]:\ProgramData\ Application Data\VMware\VDM\logs`.

For the Connection Server and the Security Server, the PCoIP Gateways log their traffic into the same directory with the filenames `pcoip_agent*.log` and `pcoip_server*.log`.

You can change the log levels that are recorded by navigating to **Start | All Programs | VMware | Set View Connection Server Log Level**.

You also can change the log rotation, size, and numbers by editing the Registry setting `[HKEY_LOCAL_MACHINE\SOFTWARE\VMware, Inc.\VMware VDM\Log]`.

Please refer to the following table:

Description	Key	Default
Days logs are kept	MaxDaysKept	-
Amount of logfiles	MaxDebugLogs	10
Log file size (MB)	MaxDebugLogSizeMB	50

The logfiles of the View Composer can be found at `C:\ProgramData\VMware\View Composer\Logs\`.

In addition to this, on the View desktop that was created by View Composer, the `Sysprep` logs can be found at `%system_drive%\Windows\Temp\ vmware-viewcomposer-ga-new.log`.

The logfiles of the View Agent can be found on the View desktop VM at the following directories:

- **XP**: [install Drive]:\Documents and Settings\All Users\ Application Data\VMware\VDM\logs
- **Windows 7**: [install Drive]:\ProgramData\VMware\VDM\logs

The logfiles for the View Client are on the local drive of the Client that is connecting to the View portal.

- **XP**: C:\Documents and Settings\%username%\Local Settings\ Application Data\VMware\VDM\Logs\
- **Windows 7**: C:\Users\%username%\AppData\Local\VMware\VDM\Logs\
- **Linux**: /usr/bin/vmware-view-log-collector
    - ○ **MKS log**: /tmp/vmware-username
    - ○ **PCoIP log**: /tmp/teradici-username
- **MAC**: ~/Library/Logs/VMware View Client.log

    ~/Library/Preferences/ByHost/com.microsoft.rdc.plist

    ~/Library/Preferences/com.microsoft.rdc.plist

VMware support logs

Another aspect of security is to be able to collect and send VMware support the support bundles. One of the first things that VMware support will ask you, if you log a case, is to send them the support files. Also, the VMware support bundle function allows you to collect all needed logfiles from all the places, we have discussed in the last section, at once. You may like to back them up regularly for compliance reason.

For the View Connection, Security, and Transfer Server the collection will be started by navigating to **Start** | **All Programs** | **VMware** | **Generate View Connection Server Log Bundle**, and the bundle will be created and placed on the desktop.

The support bundles for the View Clients on Windows are collected by running C:\Program Files\VMware\VMware View\Client\DCT\support.bat.

The support bundles for the View Agent are created by running C:\Program Files\ VMware\VMware View\Agent\DCT\support.bat.

You can also collect the Agent bundles from the View Connect Server by running
`C:\Program Files\VMware\Vmware View\Server\tools\bin\vdmadmin -A`
`-getDCT -outfile file_name -d pool_name -m virtual_machine_name`.

SSL certificates

All vSphere components and for that matter all View components communicate via a secure connection using SSL certificates. The following diagram shows all the API (HTTPS SSL secured) connections between the different layers:

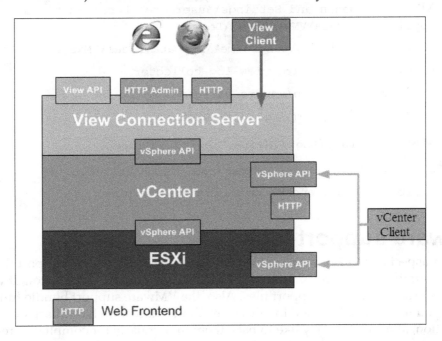

All VMware products automatically create certificates during installation. However, when using certificates that have been issued from a **Certificate Authority (CA)**, you make sure that no man-in-the-middle attack can occur. For this, we have to exchange the VMware self-signed SSL certificates that VMware uses by default with CA signed certificates.

Certificates improve not only the security for inter-server communication, but especially the client-server connectivity.

In this section we will see how we can import SSL certificates. If you don't have any trusted certificate, I will quickly show you how you get an Active Directory (AD) CA signed certificate.

Creating a Certificate Authority (CA) and obtaining a certificate

If you do not have a valid signed certificate from a trusted source, which costs money, you can build your own little CA using Active Directory. However, it is always better to use a trusted CA for business.

Creating a CA on AD

If you have a trusted certificates, skip this step.

We will now quickly create a CA on your AD server. The detailed instructions can be found here: `http://technet.microsoft.com/en-us/library/cc772393%28v=ws.10%29.aspx`.

1. Log in to your AD Server as the domain admin.
2. Open the **Server Manager** window and go to **Roles**.
3. Add the **Active Directory Certificate Services** role. Click on **Next**.
4. Select the **Certification Authority** as well as the **Online Responder** role services. This will automatically install IIS.
5. The following windows can be bypassed by clicking on **Next** (or refer to the preceding link for detailed descriptions).
6. This will install a CA on your AD.

Creating a certificate

If you have a trusted certificates, skip this step.

To generate a certificate we must first request it. There are several methods on how to do this. To request the certificate one can use the method of using Open SSL as described in the links beneath, use an online request form (`http://www.gogetssl.com/online-csr-generator`) or use the in-built Microsoft engine. We will use the last method.

1. Open an IE window on your computer that you installed CA on and go to `http://localhost/certsrv`.
2. Login with a domain administrator account.
3. Click on **Request a Certificate**.

4. Click on **Advanced Certificate Request**.

5. Click on **Create and submit a request to this CA** (this option exists only if you are on the CA server itself and use Internet Explorer).

6. Switch the certificate template to **Webserver**.

   For **Name**, enter the FQDN of the server that will host the certificates. If you do not enter the correct FQDN, the certificates will not be accepted by a Client connecting to the server as it believes you stole the certificates.

7. Fill in the other text fields as required. Leave all other options as they are.

8. Click on **Submit**.

The certificate is now issued. Now we need to download it.

1. Click on Start and in the command-line console type mmc.

2. In the MMC select **File | Add/Remove Snap-in…**.

3. Select **Certificates** and **My user account** and click on **OK**.

4. Expand **Personal | Certificates**.

5. Right-click the certificates you like to export and select **All Tasks | Export…**.

6. Export with **No Private Key**.

7. Use the **DER** format.

8. Give the file a name and save it.

9. You now have a certificate and we will proceed to import it into another server.

Importing a certificate

This step is the same for trusted and self-signed certificates.

Now we will import the certificate into our server. This step is required for any of the server installation.

1. Log in to the server that will be/is running the View Composer.

2. Click on Start and in the command line type mmc.

3. In the MMC select **File | Add/Remove Snap-in…**.

4. Select **Certificates** and **Computer Account** and click on **OK**.

5. Select **Local Computer** and click on **OK**.

6. Right-click on **Personal** and select **All Tasks | Import...**.

7. Select the saved `.cer` file.

8. Clicking on **Next** and then **Finish** will import the certificate.

Now that we have the certificates imported we can continue. Make sure your root certificate from your AD has been imported. If your server is a part of an Active Directory, this has automatically happened.

Retrofit vSphere

If you would like to replace the vSphere self-signed certificates, here are the links that will help you:

- Refer to *Configuring CA signed certificates for ESXi 5.x hosts* in VMware KB 2015499

- Refer to *Creating certificate requests and certificates for vCenter Server 5.1 components* in VMware KB 2037432

 If you have already attached a vCenter and a Composer to the View Connection server you will have to redo the vCenter configuration in View Administrator.

The View Composer

The SSL certificate for the View Composer can either be chosen during the installation of View Composer or it can be exchanged after the installation. If you plan to install View Composer on the vCenter Server, you can reuse the vCenter certificate.

Installer

1. Run the installer as usual. At some stage, the installer will ask you if you like to **Create a new SSL certificate** or **Use an existing SSL certificate**.

2. Select **Existing** and then the certificate you imported before. The following screenshot shows VMware View Composer:

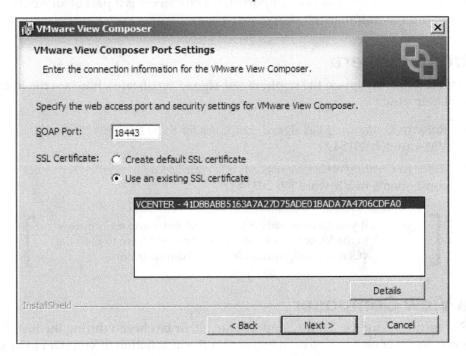

Retrofit

If you already installed the View Composer, you can retrofit a certificate to the installation. Stop the View Composer service.

1. Open a command prompt window (navigate to **Start | cmd**).

2. In the command prompt, use the `cd` command to go to the location of the View Composer installation (`c:\Program Files (x86)\VMware\VMware View Composer`).

3. Now run the `command sviconfig -operation=ReplaceCertificate -delete=false`.

4. Select the certificate you like to use by choosing the number.

5. Start the View Composer service.

The View Connection Server

For View Connection Servers and View Security Servers, we need to create a friendly name for our imported certificate.

1. In MMC, go to the imported certificate.

2. Now right-click on the certificate and select **Properties**.

3. In the box **friendly name**, write vdm and click on **OK**.

Set the friendly name only for one certificate per server.

Creating a redundant View Connection Server

We already discussed the challenge of a Virtual desktop environment, one of which is that the every desktop user is now utilizing the View Connection Server. In order to load balance, and more importantly, provide failover capability, we now will install a second copy of the View Connection Server. This chapter assumes that you already have an existing installation of a View Connection Server (Standard).

Usage of a replica server

There are several ways that a replica View Connection Server can be used. The first and the most straightforward method is to use it to serve specialized desktop pools. The replica and the standard View Connection Server have different IPs, but will share the same ADAM base as well as the same basic configuration. Publishing two different IPs to two different kinds of personnel will automatically lead to "hardcoded" load balancing; meaning that one specific group of people will only ever use one View Connection Server to connect to. However, both groups can have access to all desktop pools. You can set what desktop pool can be used by what connection group when creating the desktop pool. The following screenshot shows the Add Pool dialog box where a pool can be limited to specified View Connection Servers:

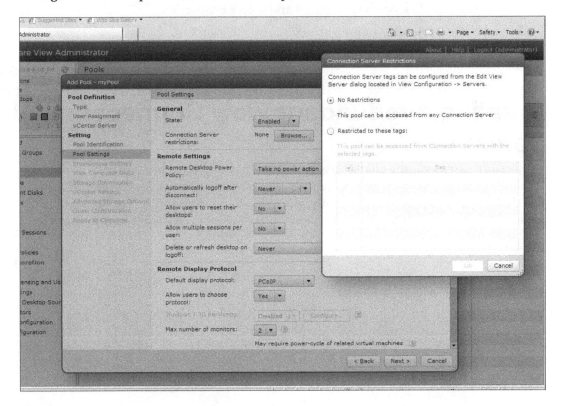

Additionally, when installing the View Client, a default View Connection Server can be chosen (refer to *Chapter 4, Securing the Client*).

This principle can be used to separate, for example, thin client and View Client workloads from each other, separate locations, departments, and so on.

This gets more interesting when we assume that the replica server is dedicated for external desktop users and is connected to the Security Server in the DMZ, whereas the standard server is used for local desktop users. This is a common security principle to make sure that the external workload follows a certain path. This setting can secure the distribution between local and external workloads and make logging of incidents easier, as it is clear what workload is going to which View Connection Server. Also, think about the usage of VLAN tunneling between the DMZ-based View Security Server and the View Connection Server; we will discuss this in *Chapter 3, Securing the Connection*.

To create a HA or load balanced View pool, we have to use a load balancer in front of the View Connection Servers. VMware View doesn't provide this; however, any commercial load balancer will do (for example, F5). **VMware Network and Security (vNS alias vShield)** in the Advanced Version can support this as well. In a load balanced scenario, the **Virtual IP (VIP)** is used to publish the View portal and clients connect to it and are redirected to one of the View Connection Servers as shown in the following diagram:

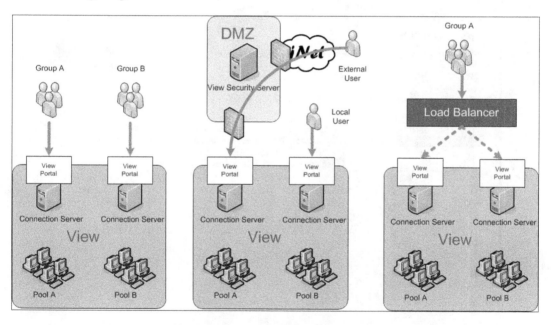

Both the scenarios can be combined to create a load balanced View connection for external and for local desktop users. We will talk about that in the next chapter. We will now install a replica server and then talk about load balancing it.

Installation of a replica server

Now we will install the secondary View Connection Server (replica).

1. Create a new VM for the View Connection Server. Make sure that you follow the hardware and software specifications.
2. In vSphere make sure that you add an anti-affinity rule to your cluster to make sure that when an ESXi Server fails, only one of the View Connection Server fails with it.
3. **Optional step:** Create a new SSL certificate and import it into the server (refer to *SSL certificates*).
4. Start the View Connection Sever installer.
5. Accept the licensing agreement and select the path for the installation of files.
6. Select **View Replica Server**. The following screenshot shows the VMware View Connection Server setup window:

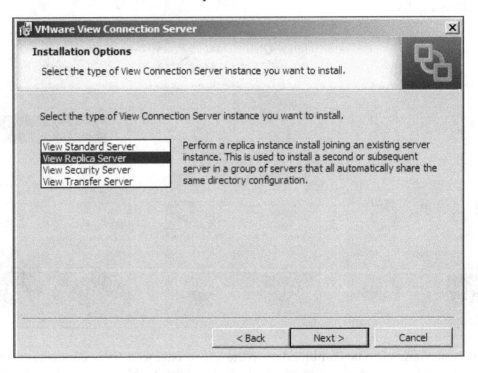

7. Enter the FQDN of the first View Connection Server you installed as shown in the following screenshot:

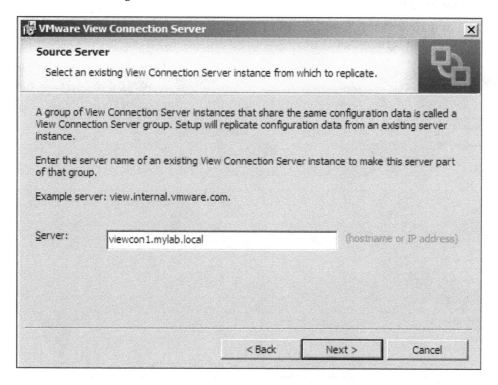

8. Choose to have the firewalls configured automatically.
9. Finish the installation process.

After the Installation has finished, do the following:

1. Log in to the View Administrator interface.

2. Navigate to **View Configuration** | **Servers** as shown in the following screenshot:

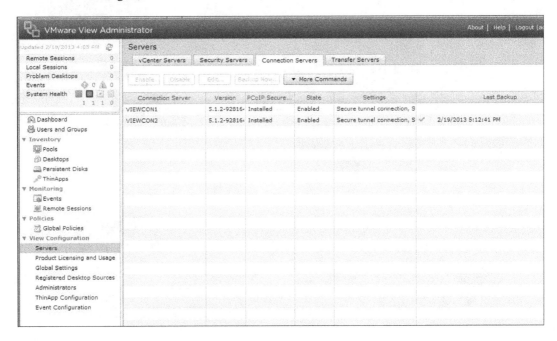

You should now see that there are two Connection Severs assigned to this View environment.

The next test we should do is connecting to the new replica server using the View Client. Perform the following steps for this:

1. Open the View Client.
2. Type in the hostname or the IP of the replica server.

You should now have access to all the View desktop pools you configured earlier.

Creating a load balanced View Connection Server

The basic idea of load balancing the View Connection Server is to load balance the access of the View portal. This also means that for the intention of load balancing the View Connection Serves (for load balancing View Security Servers refer to *Chapter 3, Securing the Connection*), we actually only need to load balance the access to the View portal on port 443. Port 80 is an auto forward to port 443. The PCoIP will then be bound to the View Connection Server we request the desktop from. The connection details are explained in *Chapter 3, Securing the Connection* in more detail.

As there are quite a lot of different load balancers, each with their different setup method, we will discuss how to set up a load balancer in general and then I will give links to specific setup examples on the Internet. Please be aware that most Internet examples deal with a load balanced scenario for the View Security Servers.

The general steps to configure a load balancer for View Connection Server are:

- **Define the virtual servers**: These are the two View Connection Servers.
- **Define the load-balanced ports**: This is basically port TCP 443 (HTTPS) and if you want port TCP 80 (HTTP), you can use it.
- **Define the virtual server**: This is the IP that the load balancer will present to View Client connections. The following settings should be implemented.

Protocol	TCP Port	Persistent Method
HTTP	80	Cookie
HTTPS	443	SSL_Session_ID

The important point here is the "stickiness" (persistent method); we want to use SSL forwarding and make sure that we stay on the same server using the SSL session ID.

- **Health check options**: A good way to set a health check is to set the HTTP service to check on `[view connection server IP]?page=noclient.jsp`.

Here now some specific links on how to configure different load balancers:

- Refer to `http://www.2vcps.com/2010/04/26/using-network-load-balancing-with-view` to configure Microsoft NBL Service

- Refer to `http://virtualfuture.info/2012/02/free-load-balancing-for-vmware-view-with-citrix-netscaler-vpx-express/` to configure Citrix NetScaler

- Refer to `http://www.f5.com/pdf/white-papers/dell-f5-vmware-view-wp.pdf` to configure F5

- `http://load balancer.org/pdffiles/Load balancer-orgQuickGuide-VMwareView.pdf`

This concludes the load balancer section for View Connection Severs. Note that in the next chapter, we will come back to this discussing the load balancing of the View Security Servers. The load balancing of the View Security Server is more widely discussed on the Internet than the load balancing of the View Connection Server. The reason for this is that even in an organization that doesn't expose their View infrastructure to the Internet, they might choose to use the View Security Server to secure their View infrastructure internally.

A configuration example with vCloud Network and Security (vCNS or vShield)

We will now run through an example setup of a load balancer for the View Connection Server. This same example also works with the View Security Server.

For this example, we need two View Connection Servers: a vCNS (Advanced License) appliance and a deployed edge as shown in the following diagram:

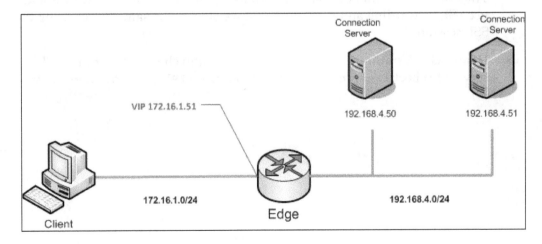

We can now configure the load balancing part of the edge.

1. Log in to the vCNS Manager.

2. Navigate to **Datacenter** and click on the datacenter you have configured the edge in.

3. Navigate to **Network Virtualization | Edge** and double-click on the edge you have deployed.

4. Navigate to **Load Balancer | Pools**.

5. We are now defining the pools. Click on the green **+** button.

6. Give the pool a name (no spaces) and check the box for **HTTPS** as shown in the following screenshot:

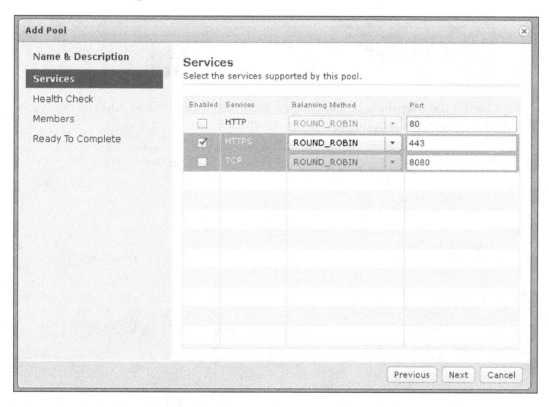

Under the **Health Check** block, just enter /?page=noclient.jsp as shown in the following screenshot:

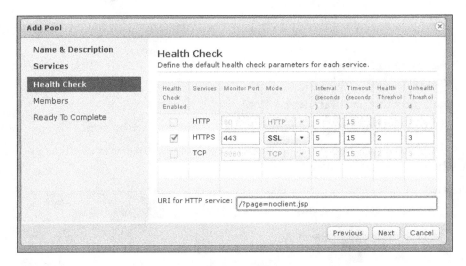

Under the **Members** block, click on the green **+** button and add the two View Severs as shown in the following screenshot:

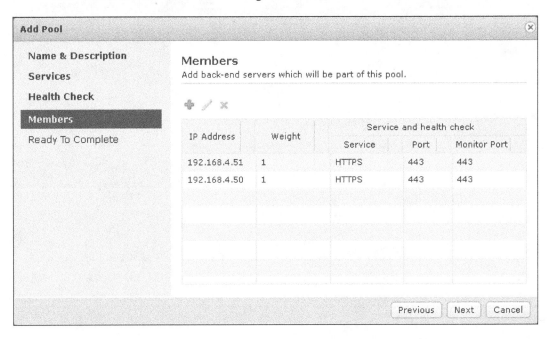

7. Complete the wizard by clicking on **Finish**.
8. Click on **Publish Changes** in the green bar.

9. Now click on **Virtual Servers** as shown in the following screenshot:

   We are now adding the VIP (or external IP) that the client will be connecting to. Click on the green + button.

10. Enter a name for the VIP.

11. Enter the IP you want to have as the load balancer IP.

12. Select the pool you created earlier.

13. Select **HTTPS** and make sure you select SSL_SESSION_ID as the persistence method.

14. Click on **Add** to close the dialog.

15. Again click on **Publish Changes** in the green bar.

16. Again click on **Pools**.

17. Click on **Enable** and then on **Publish Changes**.

This concludes the setup of the load balancer. If you are using a View Security Server, you should now configure the View HTTPS or PCoIP gateway address as explained the *The desktop connection* section in *Chapter 3, Securing the Connection*.

Summary

You should now understand more about the base services of View as we have looked at the vSphere aspects of clustering and talked about logs and SSL certificates. We have also discussed creating View replica servers and load balancing them to create a stable and redundant setup.

In the next chapter, we look at connections between the base and the client. We will discuss the desktop connections with the different View desktop protocols we can use, as well as taking a look at the View Security Server and the View Transfer Server.

3
Securing the Connection

In this chapter we will concentrate on securing the connection. What this means is the connection between the View Client and the View desktop as well as all the connections in between.

View connections

We will now discuss how View establishes a connection and how the View desktops work. The View connection is basically broken down into three components.

- The View Agent that is installed on the VM, that is, the source for the desktops

- The View Client that is installed on a remote PC, Mac, thin client, or other devices that are receiving the remote desktop

- The last and third part is the View connector that acts as a connection broker and lets the View Client choose a View desktop, and connects it to the View Agent

The View Client will by default try to establish a direct connection between the View Client and the View Agent/desktop using either RDP or PCoIP as a desktop protocol. We will later learn how to configure a secure HTTPS or PCoIP Secure Gateway connection between them.

A View DMZ

A **DMZ (demilitarized zone)** is a buffer zone between the internal network that contains sensitive data and hosts, and an outside unsecure network with potential danger. In a DMZ, a **View Security Server** forwards traffic to the **View Connection Server**, therefore hiding it and its entire depending infrastructure from the outside. We will discuss the details of the View Security Server in one of the next sections. The important point to be understood at this stage is that each View Security Server is paired with one View Connection Server. This means that if one is creating multiple DMZ's or load-balanced security servers, more View Connection Servers have to be created, resulting in addition of resources used for the management part of View. Most people will place a DMZ between the internal network and the Internet. However, in case of View, not only can the Internet be an unsecure network, but the internal network could be considered unsecure. Depending on your security concerns, you may want to secure the View environment against the internal network; therefore, creating a DMZ between the View environment and the internal network is a good idea. It is possible to create multiple DMZ's for View. This is due to the fact that each View Connection-Security Server pairing can be configured with an external URL for connection. Instead of a View DMZ, the usage of the HTTP(s) secure tunnel (for RDP) or the PCoIP Gateway (for PCoIP) can reduce the number of open ports needed between the View Client and the View desktop.

View Security Server

We now turn our attention to the View Security Server. The security server exists as a way to expose the View desktop to a less secure environment; for example, the Internet. Each View Security Server is paired with one View Connection Server and acts as a proxy for all connection.

In the newest version, the security server has the ability to proxy the View HTTPS (RDP) as well as the PCoIP connections between the external client and the portals. Before View 4.6, PCoIP was not a very good choice for View desktops; neither the View Security Server nor the View Connection Server was able to proxy the PCoIP connection. Meaning, that the external client needed a direct connection (and DNS resolution) to the View desktop, therefore, opening up the internal structures to the external network.

The PCoIP Gateway service securely connects the client and View desktop making PCoIP now a valid and secure choice for an external desktop protocol.

As I mentioned earlier, one View Security Server can only be paired with one View Connection Server, however, you can point multiple View Security Servers at the same View Connection Server. This setup is handy if you have multiple DMZs that connect to the same core View environment. Please be aware that if you are connecting multiple View Security Servers to a single View Connection Server, you are creating a single point of failure. The following diagram explains the setup:

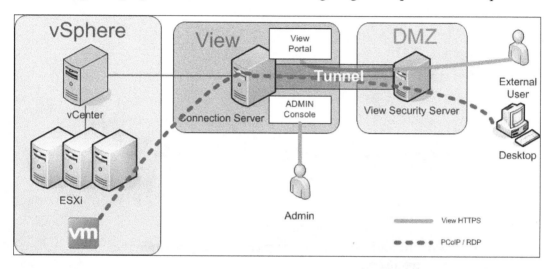

To configure these setting see the *Setting up PCoIP Secure Gateway* section later in this chapter.

Setup

Let's set up the View Security Server as shown in the following steps:

The prerequisite for setting up a View Security Server is an existing View Connection Server. We will start by preparing the View Connection Server for pairing. Be aware that the pairing password has a time limit, which can be set, but remember it needs to be used in this allocated time frame. The pairing password has to be entered during the installation of the security server software.

1. Log in to the View Administration console.
2. Navigate to **View Configuration | Servers**.
3. Select the View Connection Server that should be used as the target for the security server.

4. Select **Specify Security Server Pairing Password** from **More Commands**; check the following screenshot for reference:

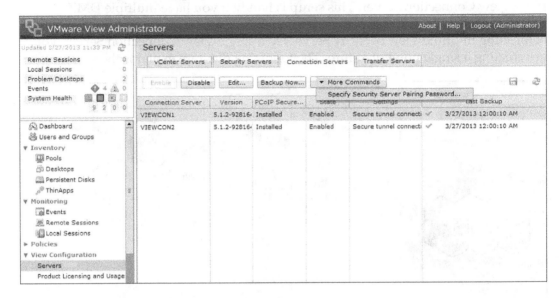

5. Set a password and validity for the password as shown in the following screenshot:

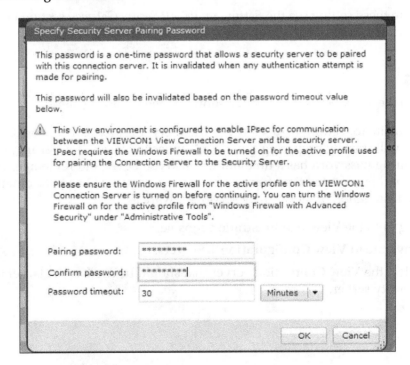

6. Click on the **OK** button.

We now go on to install the security server software as shown in the following steps:

1. Log in to the Windows server.

2. Create a new SSL Cert and import it into the server (see *Chapter 2, Securing Your Base*). This step is *optional* but is *highly recommended*.

3. Start the View connect installation.

4. Accept the licensing agreement and select the path for the installation files.

5. Select the path for the installation.

6. Select **View Security Server** as done in the following screenshot:

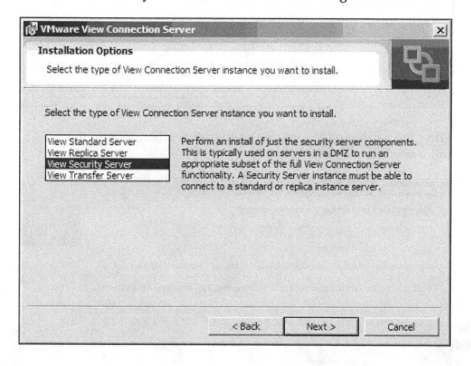

7. Enter the IP or the FQDN of the View Connection Server that this View Security Server should be paired with as shown in the following screenshot:

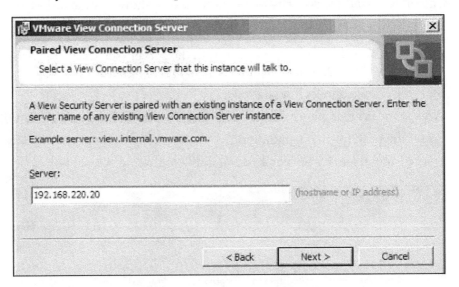

8. Enter the pairing password you configured earlier, refer to the following screenshot:

9. In **External URL**, enter the URL a client would be connecting to. If you are using a load balancer in front of the View Connection Server, enter that URL. The URL consists of the protocol and the port; for example, `https://myview.mylab.local:443`. Now enter the external PCoIP URL. It is always the IP of the security server followed by the PCoIP port (`4172`); for example, `192.168.1.50:4172` as shown in the following screenshot:

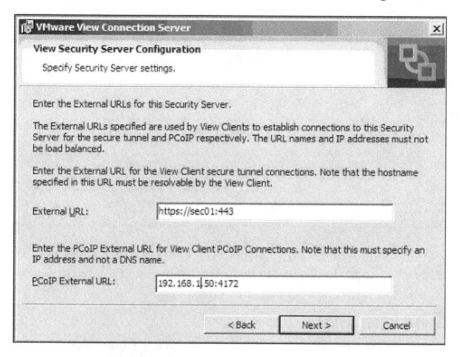

10. Choose the way the setup should configure the Windows firewalls.
11. Complete the installation.

Switch back to the View admin console and navigate to **View Configuration |
Servers | Security Servers**, refer to the following screenshot:

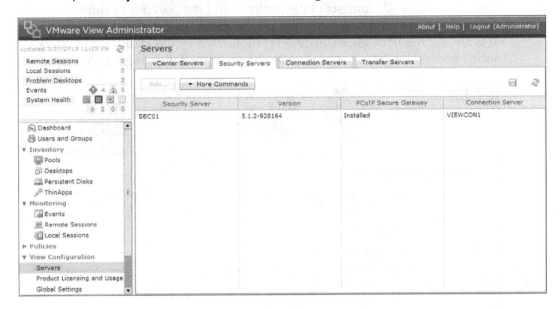

You have now configured a security server that is paired with a connection server.
You should now also try to connect to the security sever and a View desktop.

Load balancing

Because the View Security Servers are paired to the View Connection Servers there is
an impact on the design of the load balancing. The load balancing now is done in the
DMZ instead of the internal network and will just load balance TCP port 443 toward
the View Security Servers as shown in the following diagram:

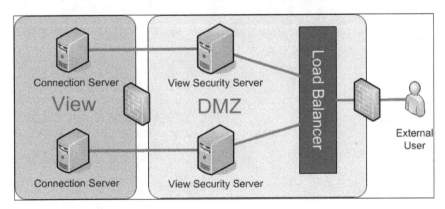

The setup of load balancing strictly follows the same procedure that we discussed in *Creating a load balanced View Connection Server*, *Chapter 2*, *Securing Your Base*. The only exception is the configuration of the HTTP(s) secure tunnel, external and the PCoIP URL. These settings have to be adjusted for load balancing, please see the *HTTP(s) secure tunnel* and *Setting up PCoIP Secure Gateway* sections in this chapter.

If you are deploying multiple security servers, it is important to create a DRS anti-affinity rule to make sure that an ESXi failure will not affect the load balancer.

General connection settings

There are several settings that can be configured to define the connection behavior. All of these settings are changed via View Administrator. The first set of these can be found by navigating to **View Configuration** | **Global Settings** as shown in the following screenshot:

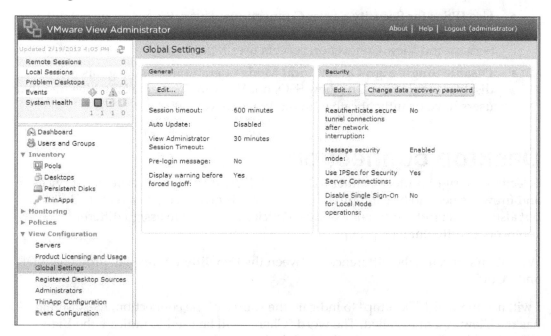

The following settings are of importance:

- **Session timeout**: It defines how long sessions between the View Client and the View desktops are kept open if not closed by disconnect. A short session timeout will force users to reauthenticate and reinitialize the View desktop connection.

- **Auto Update**: This enables and configures auto update of the global status pane.

- **View Administrator Session Timeout**: It is the time frame for connections to the View Administrator console. The longer the session extends, the higher is the risk that a man-in-the-middle attack would be successful.

- **Reauthenticate secure tunnel connections after network interruption**: If a network rupture occurs this setting can force users to reauthenticate the connection between the View Client and the View Connection Server. This can be a good idea in high security connections to prevent a man-in-the-middle attack.

- **Message security mode**: It sets how or if the communication between View components is secured. There are three modes **Disabled, Mixed**, and **Enabled**. **Enabled** should always be used, the only exception is when View components below version 4.5 are connected to this environment.

- **Use IPSec for Security Server Connections**: This setting is on by default and should be on to make sure that the communication between View Security Servers and View Connection Servers uses IPSec.

- **Disable Single Sign-On for Local Mode operations**: Enabling this feature disables Single Sign-On (View SSO, not VMware vSphere SSO). Meaning that users have to authenticate with the View desktop OS.

Desktop connection

Selecting the right protocol, either RDP or PCoIP, is important as different services and firewalls need to be configured. Both protocols give access to a remote desktop but also have slightly different features. Policies can be set to assign different protocols to different user groups.

We will first discuss the differences between the two different display protocols RDP and PCoIP.

I will use the word "Desktop" to indicate the source of the connection, the VM that has the View Agent installed. The word "Client" will be used to indicate the View Client or thin client, the remote physical desktop.

You can set the default desktop protocol when creating the desktop pool as well as the option for users to choose a different one, refer to the following screenshot:

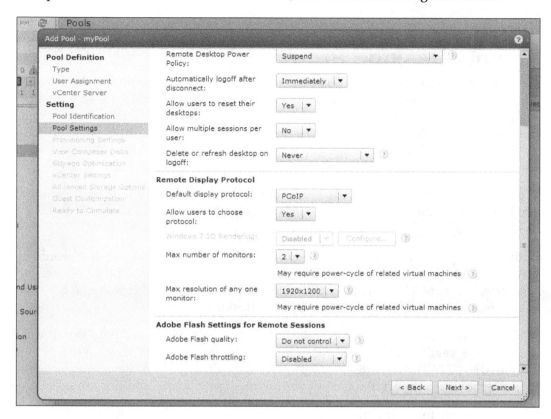

A quick look at TCP and UDP

Before we step into the PCoIP versus RDP discussion, let us review the difference between TCP and UDP. Just to clear up all misunderstanding, neither UDP nor TCP have anything to do with the addressing of packages (that's what the IP protocol is for), both are protocols to regulate how information is sent form a server to a client. TCP is a protocol that requires the receiver to acknowledge that a package has been received. If a package is not acknowledged by the client, the server will send it again until it is acknowledged. This protocol is the standard protocol for any file transfer. UDP on the other hand doesn't require an acknowledgement of packages. It just sends out packages and doesn't care if the client receives it. This protocol is used mostly for streaming media. As an example: while watching a video, the bandwidth is reduced. We now see two different reactions. With TCP the video will stop and wait until all the packages it needs have arrived and will then continue to play. With UDP the video will jump and some seconds of the video will be lost.

It is important to understand the difference between TCP and UPD, as RDP is TCP-based and PCoIP is TCP - and UDP-based. This makes PCoIP a better choice for multimedia.

Remote Desktop Protocol (RDP)

The **Remote Desktop Protocol** (Microsoft) is a standard way to connect to a Windows PC. RDP uses a Terminal Server on the desktop site that draws the desktop and presents it to the client. The main issue with this is that the refresh times depend on activity on the client site, if no activity on the client site occurs, the refresh times are cut down in order not to waste bandwidth. This can be a problem; for example, someone is watching a movie and isn't typing or constantly moving the mouse.

RDP uses a TCP (Port 3389) connection as well as desktop-side rendering. Meaning that the image of the desktop is produced on the desktop itself, adding to the load for the desktop.

With regard to USB devices, the pure RDP only supports USB hard drives, meaning that it is able to show a USB drive that was connected to the client on the desktop. However, VMware View enables USB redirection using a special connection between the VMware client and the View Agent on the desktop.

RDP comes in two versions, RDP6 and RDP7. RDP7 is implemented with Windows 7 (and newer versions), Vista and XP SP2 are configured with RDP6 (Vista can be upgraded to RDP 7). The difference between RDP 6 and RDP 7 is the amount of multiple monitor support, the quality of multimedia functions, and print redirect.

RDP is using the following ports:

Usage	From	To	Protocol	Port
RDP without tunnel	Client	Desktop	TCP	3389
RDP (tunnel)	Client	Secure, Connect	TCP	443
RDP (tunnel)	Secure, Connect	Desktop	TCP	3389

The RDP connection can be secured using the HTTP(s) secure tunnel, this security tunnel secures the connection between the client and either the secure or the connection server as shown in the following diagram:

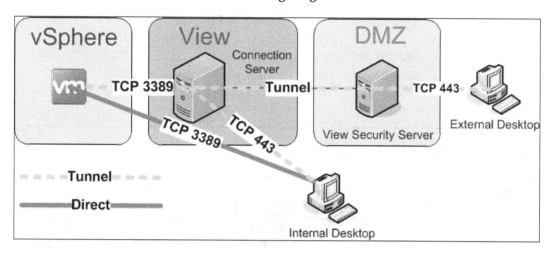

PCoverIP (PCoIP)

The PCoverIP (Teradici) was implemented early on into the View to provide an alternative to Microsoft RDP, as well as providing a fast connection for multimedia usage. PCoIP is basically an enhancement from RDP, however, there are other desktop protocols out there, but VMware currently supports RDP and PCoIP only.

The PCoIP protocol uses a UDP connection, as well as client-side rendering of the desktops. Client-side rendering means that the desktop only sends the changes in pixels across the connection and not the whole desktop picture, reducing the amount of bandwidth used as well as reducing the load on the desktop for rendering. However, this places load onto the client desktop or the thin client. It is important to understand that when thin clients would be connecting to View using PCoIP, they need a Teradici PCoIP chip.

Another interesting feature is that PCoIP can automatically adjust the image quality when network congestions occur.

One of the features that makes PCoIP more interesting is the ability of View (since version 4.6) to act as a gateway for the PCoIP connection between the client and the desktop. See also the *Setting up PCoIP Secure Gateway* section in this chapter.

PCoIP uses the following ports:

Usage	From	To	Protocol	Port
PCoIP Gateway	View Client	Security or Connect	TCP/UDP	4172
	Security or Connect	View Client	UDP	4172
	Security or Connect	View Agent (on desktop)	TCP	4172
Direct connect	View Client	View Agent (on desktop)	TCP	4172

The following diagram shows the structure:

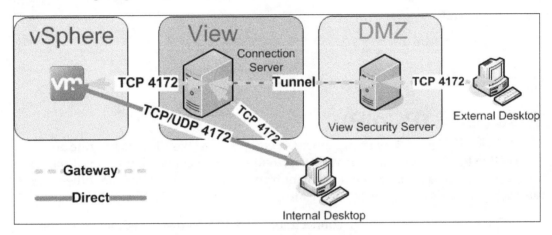

RDP and PCoIP – direct comparison

Let's list the differences between RDP and PCoIP directly next to each other:

	RDP	PCoIP
Multiple monitors	RDP6 – 2 RDP7 – 16	4 (2 with 3D)
Encryption	128 bit	128 bit
Color	32 bit	32 bit
Copy Paste	Text, images, files	Text, images
Native USB redirection	No	Yes
ClearType font	No	Yes

	RDP	PCoIP
Audio	Bi-directional	Bi-directional audio redirection with dynamic quality adjustment
Guest requirements	RDP6: XP SP2, RDP7: Vista, Windows7, Windows8, Windows 2008	XP SP2, Vista, Windows7, Windows8
Main protocol	TCP	UDP

Looking at the direct overview above the RDP seems to have better capabilities, however, the PCoIP protocol is mostly a better choice due to the fact that it has better multimedia support.

Setting up PCoIP Secure Gateway

The PCoIP Secure Gateway service was introduced in View 4.6. Previously when a View Client wanted to open a PCoIP connection he/she had open up a direct connection between the client and desktop. In the following diagram this is shown as the dash line. This means that the whole desktop infrastructure has to be exposed (or at least the PCoIP TCP, and UDP Port) to the network where the View Client lives. Since View 4.6 the View Connection Server can now act as a gateway between the View desktop and the View Client. This is shown in the following diagram as the dotted line. This allows hiding the desktop infrastructure from other networks. If the PCoIP Secure Gateway is configured, USB and MMR redirection will still use the HTTPS Secure Gateway connection. In the *Server connection* section in this chapter we will see more detailed information about the ports and protocols. The following diagram shows the structure:

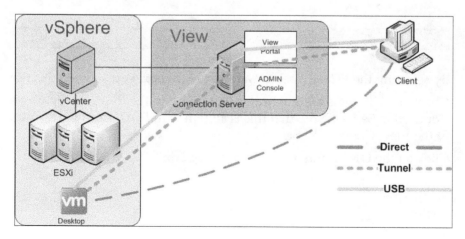

The setup is easy, however, if you are using the View Security Server we will need to also configure PCoIP Secure Gateway in the security server.

The View PCoIP Gateway isn't switched on by default. We now configure the service as shown in the following steps:

1. Log in to the View Administration console.

2. Navigate to **View Configuration | Servers | Connection Servers**.

3. Click on one of the View Connection Servers and choose **EDIT**, which will take you to a window as shown in the following screenshot:

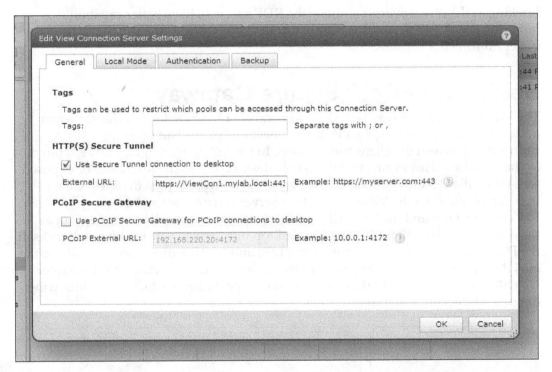

4. By selecting the **PCoIP Secure Gateway** checkbox, you activate this feature.

5. Check the URL, it is automatically configured to the IP of the View Connection Server. Note that this is an IP not an FQDN and is always the IP of the View Connection Server.

6. Click on the **OK** button to close the dialog box.

If you are not using the security server, the configuration is now finished.

If you are using a security server we need to do some additional steps. We will now configure the security server for PCoIP as shown in the following steps:

1. Navigate to **View Configuration | Servers | Security Servers**.

2. Click on one of the View Security Servers and choose **EDIT**, which will take you to a window as shown in the following screenshot:

3. Check **External URL** and adjust the settings accordingly.

4. Check **PCoIP External URL** and adjust the settings accordingly. Note that this is an IP and not an FQDN.

You now have configured PCoIP Secure Gateway and the feature is now ready to use.

If you are using a load balancer, your external URL will be the URL of the Load balancer.

HTTP(s) secure tunnel

The HTTP(s) secure tunnel provides a secure connection between the View Client and the View desktop. Without the secure tunnel the client connects directly to the desktop. The secure tunnel basically encapsulates the RDP connection. The HTTP(s) secure tunnel service is switched on by default, and can configure in the View Connection Server and the View Security Sever. To configure the HTTP(s) tunnel follow these steps:

1. Log in to the View Administration console.
2. Navigate to **View Configuration | Servers | Connection Servers**.
3. Click on one of the View Connection Servers and choose **EDIT**.
4. Check the external URL, it is automatically configured to the FQDN of the View Connection Server.

 The URL contains the HTTPS protocol as well as port 443.

5. Click on the **OK** button to close the dialog box.

If you are not using a security server, the configuration is now finished.

If you are using a security server we need to do some additional steps. We will now configure the HTTPS tunnel in the security server as shown in the following steps:

1. Navigate to **View Configuration | Servers | Security Servers**.
2. Click on one of the View Security Servers and choose **EDIT**.
3. Check the external URL and adjust the settings accordingly.
4. Check the external URL, it is automatically configured to the FQDN of the View Connection Server.

 The URL contains the HTTPS protocol as well as port 443.

If you are using a load balancer, your external URL will be the URL of the load balancer.

As this service is active by default the only time any changes must be done is when configuring a load balancer. Switching this service will result in the View Client needing a direct connection to the View desktop.

USB redirection

VMware View uses TCP port 32111 to forward the USB connection between the View Client and the View desktop for both PCoIP and RDP, even as PCoIP has USB redirection natively. This is done to separate traffic and to speed up communication.

Usage	From	To	Protocol	Port
Direct	Client	Desktop	TCP	32111
Tunnel	Client	Security or Connect	TCP	443
	Security or Connect	Desktop	TCP	32111

Multimedia redirect (MMR)

The multimedia redirect is used together with the RDP to improve multimedia performance. This is shown in the following table:

Usage	From	To	Protocol	Port
Direct	Client	Desktop	TCP	9427
Tunnel	Client	Security or Connect	TCP	443
	Security or Connect	Desktop	TCP	9427

View Transfer Server

A transfer server enables desktops in Local Mode (offline desktops in earlier editions). Desktops in Local Mode are desktops that run on the local client hardware using VMware virtualization technology. Local Mode is mostly used by people who need to use corporate desktops and have to be mobile with reduced bandwidth or non-trusted networks. This also means that the desktop has to be downloaded from the vSphere environment onto the user's machine. Furthermore, local desktops enable the check-in and check-out, meaning once the desktop has been loaded onto the client hardware the changes made in Local Mode can be replicated back to the vSphere environment. The transfer server enables this transfer. Transfer servers can either use a local drive or a shared drive to store the image. When local desktops are used in conjunction with linked clones, a shared directory must be used.

The transfer server has to be a virtual server and the vCenter that manages the transfer server has to be reachable by the View Connection Server.

Usage	From	To	Protocol	Port
Tunnel	Security	Transfer	TCP	80443
Direct	Client	Transfer	TCP	80443
JMS	Transfer	Connection	TCP	4001
Desktop replication / Check-in and out	Connect	ESXi	TCP	902
Composer packages	Transfer	ESXi	TCP	901
Composer packages	Transfer	Repository share	TCP	445

The following diagram shows the structure:

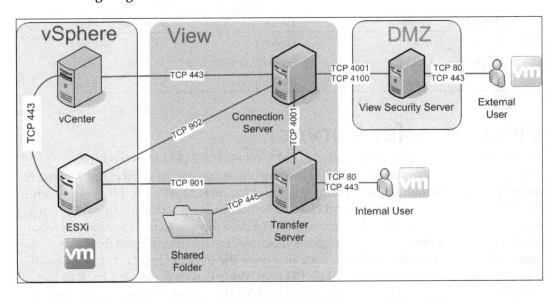

Setup

We now are installing the transfer server as shown in the following steps:

1. Start the View connect installation.

2. Accept the licensing agreement and select the path for the installation files.

3. Select the path for the installation.

4. Select **View Transfer Server** as shown in the following screenshot:

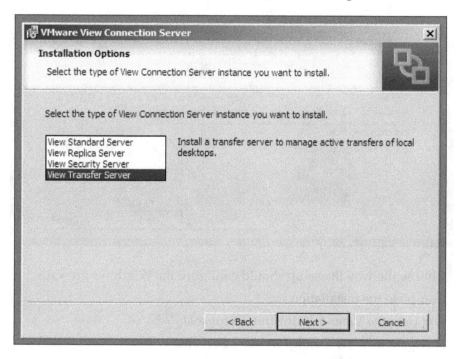

5. Check the settings for the Apache installation as shown in the following screenshot:

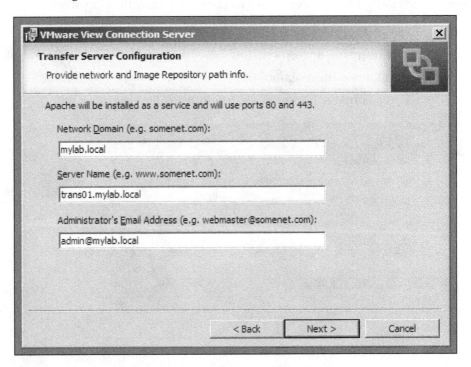

6. Choose the way the setup should configure the Windows firewalls.

7. Complete the installation.

8. Log in to the View Administration console.

9. Navigate to **View Configuration | Servers**.

10. Select the **Transfer Servers** tab as shown in the following screenshot:

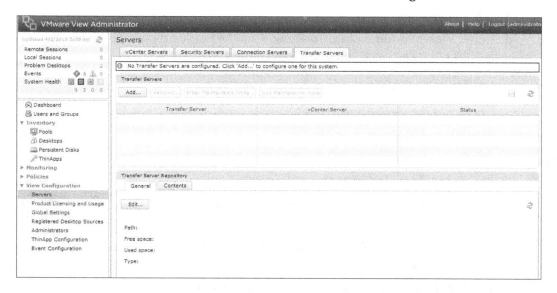

11. Click on the **Add** button.

12. Select the **vCenter Server** name that is hosting transfer server as shown in the following screenshot:

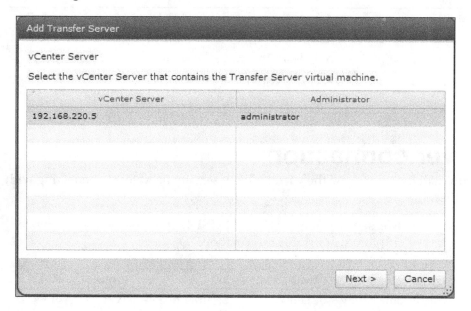

13. Select the VM that holds the transfer server.

14. Click on **Finish**.

15. In the View Administrator the View Transfer Server should now show **No Transfer Server Repository Configured**.

We now will configure the repository for the transfer server.

1. Click on **Transfer Server**.

2. Select **Enter Maintenance Mode**.

3. Click on **OK** and wait until the transfer server is in maintenance mode.

4. Make sure **Transfer Servers** is still selected and click on **Edit**.

5. Select either **Local** or **Network file system** and enter all required information.

6. Click on **OK**.

7. Make sure **Transfer Servers** is still selected and click on **Exit Maintenance Mode**.

8. The **Status** field of transfer server should now show **Ready**.

The firewalls installed during the transfer server installation are as follows:

Usage	From	To	Protocol
JMSIR	Any:Any	4100:Any	TCP
JMS	Any:Any	4001:Any	TCP
HTTPS	Any:Any	443:Any	TCP
HTTP	Any:Any	80:Any	TCP
AJP13	Any:Any	8009:Any	TCP

Server connection

We now will look into how the various View servers need to be connecting with each other.

View uses **Java Message System** (**JMS** and **JMSIR**) and Apache JServ protocol version 1.3 (AJP13) to transport this information.

Usage	From	To	Protocol	Port
Client connectivity	Client	Security or Connection	TCP	80443
JMSIR	Security	Connection	TCP	4100

Usage	From	To	Protocol	Port
JMS	Security	Connection	TCP	4001
AJP13	Security	Connection	TCP	8009
JMSIR	Replica	Connection	TCP	4100
JMS	Replica	Connection	TCP	4001
vCenter connection	Connection	vCenter	TCP	80443
View composer connection	Connection	Composer	TCP	18443

Additional ports if there is a NAT or an IPSec firewall between the security and the connect server IPSec.

Usage	From	To	Protocol	Port
IPSec negotiation	Security	Connection	UDP	500
AJP13 forward	Security	Connection	UDP	4500

The following diagram shows the structure clearly:

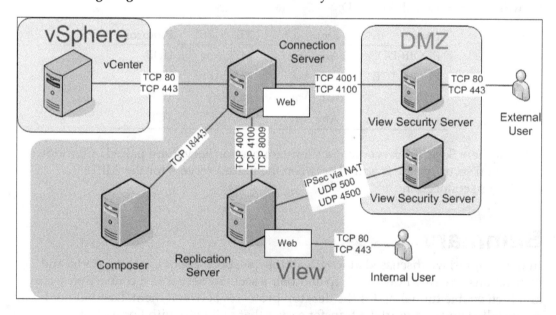

View connect and security firewall rules

During the installation of a View connect, replica, or security server the installer asks you if you like the Windows firewalls automatically configured. If you answer yes, VMware View installs automatically the inbound firewall rules and connection security rules, but no outbound rules.

View Connection Server INBOUND:

Usage	From	To	Protocol
PCOIP-UDP	Any:Any	4172:Any	UDP
PCOIP-TCP	Any:Any	4172:Any	TCP
JMSIR	Any:Any	4100:Any	TCP
JMS	Any:Any	4001:Any	TCP
HTTPS	Any:Any	443:Any	TCP
HTTP	Any:Any	80:Any	TCP
AJP13	Any:Any	8009:Any	TCP

View Security Server INBOUND:

Usage	From	To	Protocol
PCOIP-UDP	Any:Any	4172:Any	UDP
PCOIP-TCP	Any:Any	4172:Any	TCP
HTTPS	Any:Any	443:Any	TCP
HTTP	Any:Any	80:Any	TCP

When a View Security Server and a View Connection Server are paired, a Windows connection security rule is added between the paired servers for the AJP13 (TCP 8009) connection.

Summary

In this chapter, we discussed at length all the questions about protocol, ports, and connections. We saw how to set up and pair a security server to a connection server and then enable tunneling for the desktop protocols between them. Last but not least, we installed and configured a transfer server that will help with Local Mode.

In the next chapter, we will have a closer look at how to secure the client itself. We will talk about how to alter the setup process and how to use AD templates to configure USB devices and distribute security settings. We will also look into View Persona and what it can do for us.

4
Securing the Client

In this chapter we will talk about securing the View desktop client. In doing so, we need to think about securing our data and infrastructure against harmful interactions, as well as access to different environments. Harming data can take two forms, the first (and foremost) would be unauthorized alteration of data and the second, unauthorized copying of data. When you are securing your environment against data alteration and copy, you will inevitably interfere with the users' productivity. For example, if one would switch off USB forwarding, one would be saved against someone downloading data onto a USB stick, however, it would also impair any user from connecting a USB headset.

The last but most important feature is making sure that the user authenticates properly. Authentication can be as easy as logging in with an AD account or as secure as using smart cards.

In this chapter we will be talking about most of these features.

Client software

Security starts with the installation of the client software. There are two installations that are of importance. The View Agent that is installed on the View desktop template and the View Client that is installed on the client that connects to the View desktop.

View Client

The first step in securing the client is to install the View Client correctly. The View Client is available for a range of operating systems from Windows to Mac, iPad, and Android to mention the typically ones used. The first security settings can be set while installing the client. We will now run through the View Client for Windows Installer and discuss the installation options, using the following steps:

1. Execute the Installer.

2. Accept the licensing agreement.

3. Choose the features you'd like to install and select the path where you'd install the client software, as shown in the following screenshot:

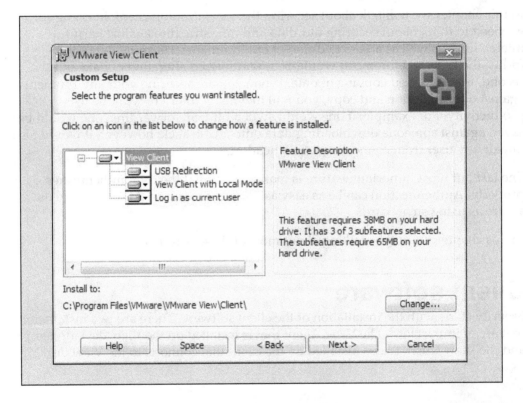

Here there are three security choices to be made (we will discuss each in detail):

 ° Enabling **USB Redirection** will enable any USB to be redirected from the client to the View desktop. Later on, in the View administrator, you can choose if you want any forwarding and even what devices should be forwarded. However, here you need to choose if *any* forwarding should occur.

- ° **View Client with Local Mode** allows users to download the View desktop to their client. A downloaded or *local View desktop* uses the local client resources (CPU, MEM, and so on) to run in an isolated space. Basically, it's like running a VM using VMware Player or VMware Workstation (Fusion on Mac).

- ° Enabling **Log in as current user** will active **Single Sign-On (SSO)**. Meaning that when the user opens a View desktop connection, the user will automatically sign in as the current user without needing additional security checks.

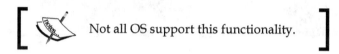 Not all OS support this functionality.

4. Chose the default View Connection Server as shown in the following screenshot:

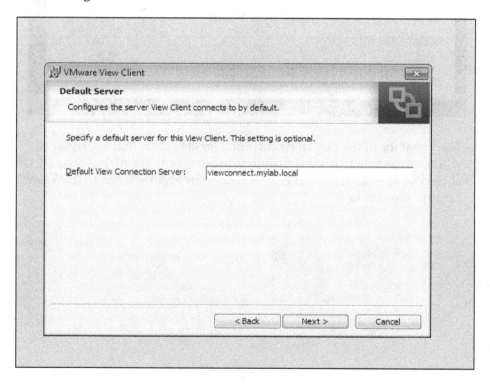

Choosing the default View Connection Server can be seen as a security feature. In *Chapter 2, Securing Your Base*, we discussed the usage of multiple View Connection Servers. This feature allows to visually "restrict" a user to a certain View Connection Server, as most users just click on **OK**.

5. Select the **Log in a current user** behavior as shown in the following screenshot:

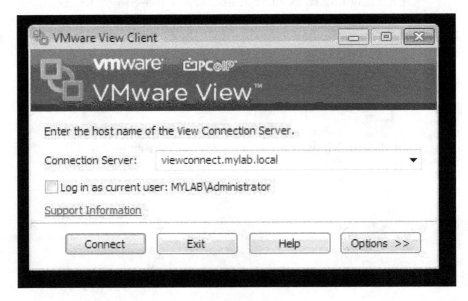

The behavior of the **Log in as current user** checkbox that is displayed when connecting to a View Connection Server can be altered. The checkbox shown in the following screenshot shows the login screens to the View Connection Server:

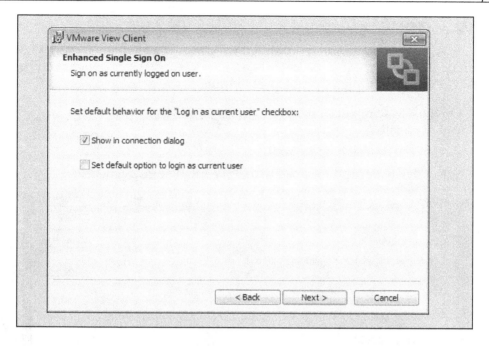

- ° **Show in connection dialog**: The **Log in as current user** checkbox is displayed. If this feature is disabled, users can not choose if they like to use Single Sign-On
- ° **Set default option to login as current user**: If this option is enabled the **Log in as current user** checkbox is ticked by default

6. Select where an icon for the View Client is displayed.
7. Review the installation path.
8. Click on **Finish**.

The important thing to understand is that the View Client can be installed silently and all the options discussed can be wrapped into an installer. This makes it possible to roll out different versions of the View Client with different security settings to various environments. The instructions to install the View Client silently are captured in the View installation guide.

More specific security settings can be set using ADM templates in AD. See the *Working with ADM templates* section in this chapter.

View Agent

The View Agent is installed on the VM that will become a template for any View desktop pool. During the installation of the View Agent, various options can be chosen. We will run through the important points now:

1. On the VM that will be the View desktop pool, execute the View Agent installer.

2. Accept the licensing agreement.

3. Select the install options as shown in the following screenshot:

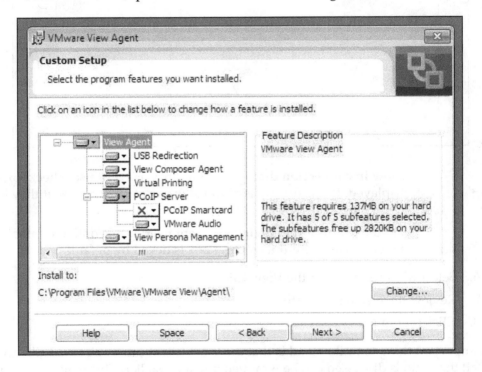

As with the View Client, several base security settings can be set here:

- **USB Redirection**: Installing this feature enables the View desktop to accept USB redirection.

- Virtual Printing: This feature enables this client to use virtual printers. This is a rather important function as some environments might not allow printing.

- **PCoIP Server**: Select this if you want to smart cards via PCoIP.

- **View Persona Management**: Select if you want to use View Persona Management.

4. Choose if you want to activate RDP on this VM as shown in the following screenshot:

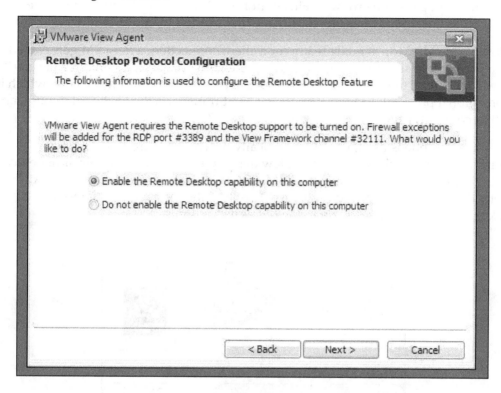

This function can be used to disable RDP as a client connection method to this View desktop template.

5. Review the installation path.

6. Finish the installation.

A common misconception is to create only one desktop template. If you are creating multiple desktop templates with different View Agent settings (for example, USB Redirect), you can improve security for certain environments, as certain functions are completely disabled.

More specific security settings can be set using ADM template in AD. See the *Working with ADM templates* section.

Local Mode

In the following sections we will talk about Local Mode, to fully understand the impact that Local Mode has on security we first needed to understand what it does.

When a View desktop is made ready for a client connection, a new VM gets cloned from the View desktop template. It runs on the vSphere environment. In a normal View connection, the View Agent transports the desktop to the View Client, which is running on a physical desktop. The View Client transports the keyboard, mouse, and USB (if configured) to the View Agent.

When Local Mode is used, the VM is basically downloaded from the vSphere environment to the client. Then, the View desktop runs on the local physical device, similarly to using VMware Player or VMware Workstation (Fusion on Mac). All interactions are now between the View Client and the local copy of the View desktop's View Agent as shown in the following diagram:

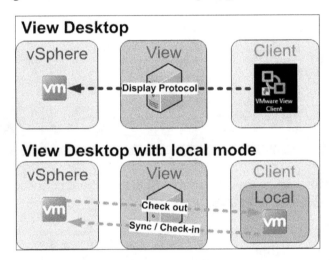

Local Mode is mostly used by staff that have to work offline or remotely with no or slow connection to a View Connection Server. A typical example is a consultant who checks out his/her View desktop in the office and then works on the files on the View Client in the plane. When the consultant can connect back to the Internet, he/she can use a View security server to sync the changes to the VM in vSphere. He/she can check the View desktop back into View, when back from office, and use the normal View Client connection to perform the work.

The benefits that Local Mode gives are clear, as are the risks. A checked-out desktop cannot be directly controlled, monitored, or disconnected. Therefore, it should be considered to create a separate View desktop pool with special VMs.

An additional concern is that each time a View desktop is checked in or out, the whole VM's hard disk must be copied between vSphere and the client. In addition to that, the more VMs that are checked out, the more syncs between the View Client and the View Agent occur. A transfer server can reduce the stress on the network and also lessen the exposer of the vSphere environment. We installed and configured a View transfer in *Chapter 3, Securing the Connection*.

In the next section we will discuss the security settings that can be set for Local Mode.

Global settings

The whole View environment can be configured with some specific settings. These settings can be accessed via **Policies | Global Policies**. These settings affect all View desktop pools, as all pools inherited these policies. Each of these policies can be overwritten by the View desktop pool settings as shown in the following screenshot:

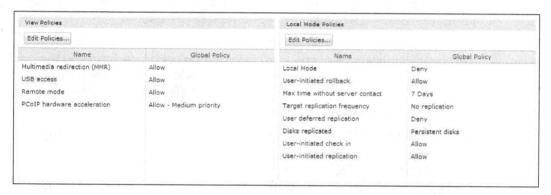

These settings fall into two sections **View Policies** and **Local Mode Policies**.

Under **View Policies** we have the following settings:

- **Multimedia redirection (MMR)**: MMR is a Microsoft DirectShow that forwards multimedia content directly to the client, which is executed on the client instead of the server. Allowing MMR redirection uses additional network ports as described in the previous chapter.

- **USB access**: This switches USB redirection on or off, even if the View Client and View Agent setting allows USB redirect.

- **Remote mode**: Disabling **Remote mode** will force users to use Local Mode, meaning that they cannot access View desktops via the View Client, but have to download the View desktop onto their client system.

- **PCoIP hardware acceleration**: This enables PCoIP hardware acceleration on devices that have a PCoIP device embedded. Typically, that is true for thin clients.

Under **Local Mode Policies** we have the following settings:

- **Local Mode**: This settings activates or deactivates Local Mode. If set to **Deny**, users cannot use Local Mode.

- **User-initiated rollback**: This setting allows users to discard their existing local copy of the View desktop. If the user initiates a rollback, all changes that have been made since the last check-in are lost. This function is useful if the downloaded copy is thought to be compromised.

- **Max time without server contact**: When a desktop is checked out, it runs only for the amount of time specified in this setting. If no connection is made during that time, the downloaded copy of the desktop will stop working. This setting is very important when a laptop is stolen. The setting can be set to unlimited, however, this might be a huge security risk.

- **Target replication frequency**: This is the amount of time between the server-side-initiated replications of changes on the downloaded desktop and the server image. If set to **No Replication**, no server-side-initiated replication will take place, however, a replication can be initiated manually from the View Administration Console or the View Client.

- **User deferred replication**: This setting allows a user to stop the currently occurring replications. This setting is useful when replications chew up network bandwidth when the user needs it.

- **Disks replicated**: This setting specifies which disks are replicated. It only applies to linked-cloned disks.

- **User-initiated check in**: This allows users to initiate a check-in from their View Client.

- **User-initiated replication**: This allows users to initiate replications from their View Client.

Desktop pools can overwrite these settings; for more information refer to the following section.

View desktop pools

The source for every View desktop is a View desktop pool. In this chapter we will discuss how to set security settings for a desktop pool.

The first thing we need to do is create a desktop pool. For the purpose of this book, we assume that you know how to do this. Now we have to access the settings of each pool, by clicking on **Inventory | Pool** and then double-clicking on the pool of which you want to change the settings. This opens up the configuration details for the pool. Every procedure that we will be performing in this section will start from here.

The Settings tab

In **Settings**, all the settings of the desktop pool can be changed as well as the **Delete Pool...** setting. We also can change the entitlements for the pool. The **Entitlements...** setting allows us to define what user group can access this pool. All these are shown in the following screenshot:

The Inventory tab

The inventory shows all deployed View desktops, the version of their View Agent, the host they are deployed on, as well as the user currently using it. There is a second panel for ThinApps that are used; however, this is out of scope for this book. The following screenshot shows my pool:

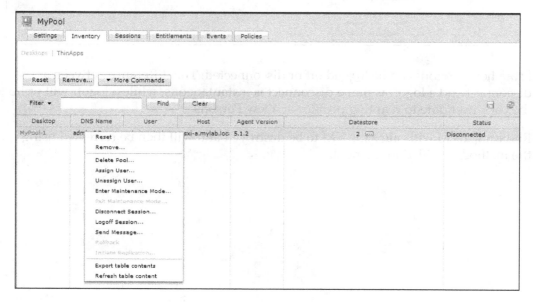

Each VM can be remotely controlled from here. This is the first place where security issues occur. User sessions can be remotely logged off or disconnected, messages can be sent to the desktop of the user/users can be assigned to special VMs. Assigning a user to a VM can be useful if the user is suspected of wrongdoing. This VM can be a special version of the normal pool VM, but with the logging and monitoring software installed on it in order to investigate or log the behavior of this user.

Putting a VM into maintenance can be used to exclude the VM from the VM Pool for example, install extra software or repair the VM.

The Sessions tab

All open sessions are shown here, with the start time, the display protocol used, as well as the duration of the session. The important thing is that it also shows through which (if any) security server the session was established as shown in the following screenshot:

From here sessions can be logged off or disconnected. The difference between a disconnect and a logoff is that a disconnect is instantaneous, while a logoff will write the back user date to roaming profiles or View Persona.

Resetting a VM will cause the VM to be destroyed and will then be recreated using the method specified in the pool.

The Entitlements tab

The entitlements for View desktops can be set at multiple places. Entitlements assign users or groups to desktop pools. This is the most basic security setting as it defines which users can use what pool. When creating multiple pools for different environments, entitlements help us define what users can access as shown in the following screenshot:

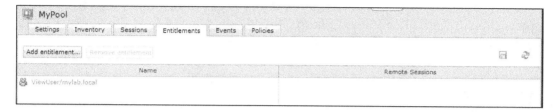

There are basically two ways to manage user-to-pool assignments. The first way is to create an AD group per View desktop pool and add this single group to the pool. This way the pool membership is managed by the AD Administrators. The second one is to add all users separately to the View desktop pool. This way is quite messy as a lot of users may need to be imported; however, pool membership is then managed by the View Administrators and not by the AD Administrators.

The Events tab

The **Events** tab shows all events that have occurred relating to the current View desktop pool. There are several filters that can be used to find specific events as shown in the following screenshot:

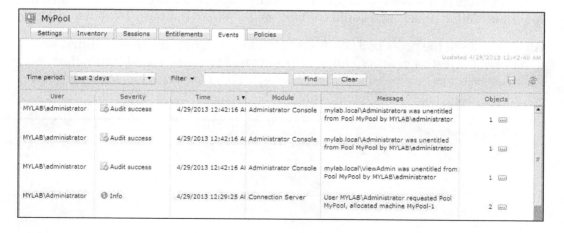

All events can be exported (the disk symbol on the right-hand side) in the `.cvs` format for further analysis. Also, if an event-db has been configured, all the events are stored there too.

The Policies tab

For each pool the global settings of the View and Local Mode policies can be overwritten. By default, a View desktop pool inherits policies from the global settings as shown in the following screenshot:

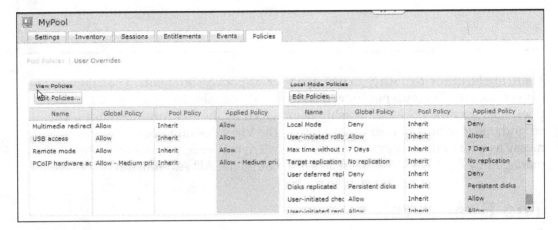

This enables the creation of specific pools, for example, a pool for "normal" View desktops and a pool only for Local Mode VMs. As each pool can be assigned to different users and VM templates, a "Local Only Pool" could be made available only to certain staff members and could contain smaller-sized, but more hardened, VMs.

All users inherit the pools policies. If you have to give a user different settings, you don't have to create a new pool for every individual user, you can simply adjust the policy settings on a per user base. Clicking on **User Overrides** and specific the settings as shown in the following screenshot:

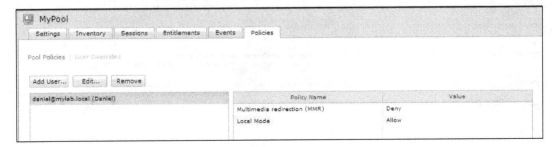

Working with ADM templates

VMware View 5.1 comes with preconfigured templates for the AD Group Policies. These policies are ADM templates and can rule out very complex security settings easily across a lot of desktops.

Importing View ADM templates

The first thing we have to do is import the ADM templates into the AD Group Policies.

- Finding the ADM template on the View Connection Server:

  View comes with preconfigured templates for AD, we now retrieve the ones for View Persona, using the following steps:

  1. Connect to your View Connection Server.
  2. Browse to the `c:\Program Files\VMware\VMware View\Server\extras\GroupPolicyFiles` folder.
  3. Copy the `*.adm` file to your AD server or any directory you can later gain access to.

- Adding the ADM template to your Group Policies:

  By adding the ADM template to the Group Policies we can re-use it more easily. Perform the following steps in order to do so:

  1. Log in to your AD server.
  2. Open **Group Policy Management (Start | Administrative Tools | Group Policy Management)**.
  3. Expand your domain and find **Group Policy Objects**.

4. Right-click on **Group Policy Objects** and select **New** as shown in the following screenshot:

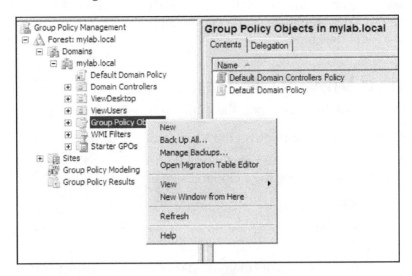

5. Name the new GPO, take for example, `View Persona`.

6. Right-click on the newly created GPO and select **edit**.

7. Expand **Computer Configuration | Policies**.

8. Right-click on **Administrative Templates** and select **Add/Remove Template...** as shown in the following screenshot:

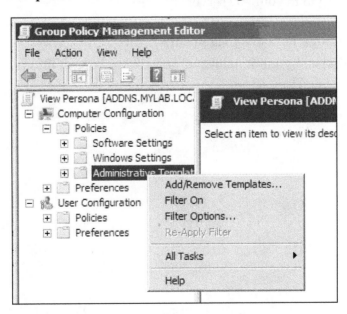

9. Now select **Add** and browse to the location where you stored the
   *.adm file. Then select **close**.

We will re-use this procedure to import the different predefined ADM templates.

View Agent settings

The View Agent has a lot of extra security settings. For that we have to import the
ADM template, by performing the following steps:

1. Copy the VDM_Agent.adm file to the AD server and add it to the Group
   Policies. Name it VDM Agent.

2. Configure the View Agent GPO. Now we can configure the View
   Agent settings. Expand **Policies | Administrative Templates | Classic
   Administrative Templates | VMware View Agent Configuration** as
   shown in the following screenshot:

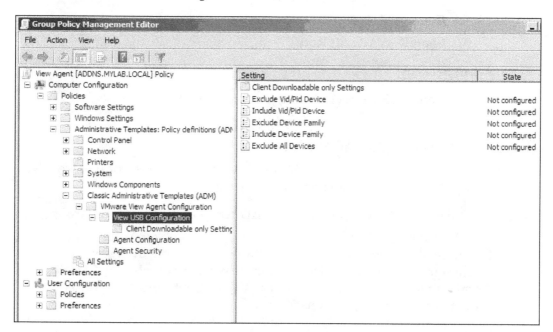

The following settings can be configured:

- **View USB Configuration**
    - **Exclude Vid/Pid Device**
    - **Include Vid/Pid Device**
    - **Exclude Device Family**

- ○ **Include Device Family**
- ○ **Exclude All Devices**

- • **Agent Configuration**
  - ○ **Force MMR to use software overlay**
  - ○ **Enable multi-media acceleration**
  - ○ **Allow Single Sign-On**
  - ○ **Connection TicketTimeout**
  - ○ **CredentialFilterExemptions**
  - ○ **Connect using DNS Name**
  - ○ **Disable Time Zone Synchronization**
  - ○ **Toggle Display Settings Control**
  - ○ **CommandsToRunOnConnect**
  - ○ **CommandsToRunOnReconnect**
  - ○ **ShowDiskActivityIcon**

- • **Agent Security**

  - ○ **Accept SSL encrypted framework channel**

View Client settings

As View Agent, the View Client has a lot of extra security settings. For that we have to import the ADM template, using the following steps:

1. Copy the `VDM_Client.adm` file to the AD server and add it to the Group Policies. Name it `VDM Client`.

2. Configure the View Agent GPO. Now we can configure the View Agent settings. Expand **Policies** | **Administrative Templates** | **Classic Administrative Templates** | **VMware View Client Configuration** as shown in the following screenshot:

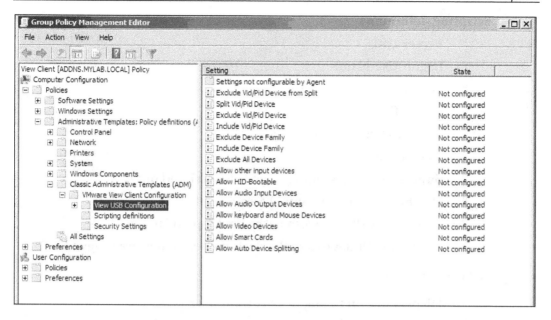

The following settings can be configured:

- **View USB Configuration**
    - ◦ **Exclude Vid/Pid Device from Split**
    - ◦ **Exclude Vid/Pid Device**
    - ◦ **Include Vid/Pid Device**
    - ◦ **Exclude Device Family**
    - ◦ **Include Device Family**
    - ◦ **Exclude All Devices**
    - ◦ **Allow other input devices**
    - ◦ **Allow HID-Bootable**
    - ◦ **Allow Audio Input Devices**
    - ◦ **Allow Audio Output Devices**
    - ◦ **Allow keyboard and Mouse Devices**
    - ◦ **Allow Video Devices**
    - ◦ **Allow Smart Cards**
    - ◦ **Allow Auto Device Splitting**

- **Scripting definitions**
    ◦ **Server URL**
    ◦ **Logon UserName**
    ◦ **Logon DomainName**
    ◦ **Logon Password**
    ◦ **DesktopName to select**
    ◦ **DesktopLayout**
    ◦ **Supress error messages (when fully scripted only)**
    ◦ **Disable 3rd-party Terminal Services plugins**
    ◦ **Connect all USB devices to the desktop on launch**
    ◦ **Connect USB devices to the desktop when they are plugged in**

- **Security Settings**
    ◦ **Display option to Log in as currant user**
    ◦ **Default value of the 'Log in as current user' checkbox**
    ◦ **Servers Trusted For Delegation**
    ◦ **Ignore certificate revocation problems**
    ◦ **Certificate verification mode**
    ◦ **Enable Single Sign-On for smart card authentication**
    ◦ **Enable jump list integration**
    ◦ **Allow command line credentials**
    ◦ **Enable SSL encrypted framework channel**

Working with USB devices

Using the ADM templates, USB devices can be filtered for USB redirection. This is configured using either the View Client or the View Agent ADM templates as we saw previously. The USB settings can be applied for single devices or device families.

To find the Vendor ID (**VID**) or Product ID (**PID**) of an USB device, perform the following steps:

1. Connect the USB device to a computer.
2. Open **Device Manager**.
3. Right-click on the **Device** you attached and select **Properties**.

4. Select the **Details** tab and select under **Property**, select **Hardware Ids** as shown in the following screenshot:

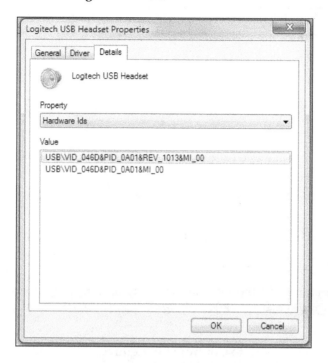

5. The VID/PID from the preceding example is **VID_046D&PID_0A01**.

The following table lists all USB family names that View 5.1 understands:

Device family name	Description
Audio	Any audio-input or audio-output device
audio-in	Audio-input devices such as microphones
audio-out	Audio-output devices such as loudspeakers and headphones
bluetooth	Bluetooth-connected devices
Comm	Communications devices such as modems and wired networking adapters
Hid	Human interface devices excluding keyboards and pointing devices
hid-bootable	Human interface devices that are available at boot time excluding keyboards and pointing devices
Imaging	Imaging devices such as scanners
keyboard	Keyboard device

Device family name	Description
Mouse	Pointing device such as a mouse
Other	Family not specified
Pda	Personal digital assistants
Physical	Force feedback devices such as force feedback joysticks
Printer	Printing devices
Security	Security devices such as fingerprint readers
smart-card	Smart card devices
Storage	Mass storage devices such as flash drives and external hard disk drives
unknown	Family not known
Vendor	Devices with vendor-specific functions
Video	Video-input devices
Wireless	Wireless networking adapters
Wusb	Wireless USB devices

More information about USB polies can be found at `http://pubs.vmware.com/view-51/index.jsp?topic=%2Fcom.vmware.view.administration.doc%2FGUID-A43F5E8E-2A15-4B2E-A1CE-FAB002FEEF8D.html`.

Or, search for "Using Policies to Control USB Redirection." In addition to that there is a good KB 1011600 that explains how USB filtering and splitting works.

View Persona management

When a user logs in to a Windows operating system, the user logs in to a local profile. This profile manages where documents, user-specific settings and files are stored and makes sure they are secured against other users. These profiles can be stored centrally using remote profiles. When a user logs on to the Windows system, the remote profile is copied from the central storage unit to the Windows system. When the user logs off, the profile, with all the changes, gets copied back to the central storage unit. This has several disadvantages; first of all a user profile can grow rather large and the time needed for the transfer can take some time, this is especially true when a large number of users log on or off at the same time, for example, in the morning. Another disadvantage is that if the user doesn't log off, but the connection is interrupted, the profile is not copied back to the central storage unit and all the changes are lost. When the network bandwidth is reduced to accommodate for profile copies we talk about a boot storm.

View Persona is an alternative to roaming profiles as it performs the
following operations:

- Copies only the files that are currently used to the View desktop, making
  logins faster. Roaming profiles copy all the files.

- Syncs the local user profile by default every 10 minutes. Roaming profiles
  sync only on logoff.

- Copies only the changes back, making the logoff faster. In roaming profiles,
  all files are written back.

- View Persona can be used with a physical non-View-managed desktop.
  However, this option is out of scope for this book but is described in the
  View Administration guide.

View Persona improves security as it reduces the load on the network during high
log on/off periods (morning and evening). It also provides a secure and individual
desktop experience that follows the user around. As remote profiles, View Persona
allows for folder redirection. This fact shouldn't be underestimated, as most users
will find workarounds to access their data that could breach security.

For a given OU, in AD you can either use Microsoft Remote Profiles or View
Persona, you cannot use both at the same time.

We will now install and configure View Persona. For this example installation, we
assume that Windows 7 desktops are used and no roaming profiles exist. It also
assumes you followed the setup recommendations and created a View desktop OU.

The installation is basically rather easy and straightforward. We create a share
directory and then apply an AD Group Policy template (ADM template) to the
View desktop OU in AD. Configuration is done by activating the Group Policy and
entering the shared path, as given in the following steps:

1. In order to make View Persona work we have to create a storage share where
   the profile will be stored:

   1. Create a CIFS/SMB (Windows Share) shared directory and
      hide the share by adding a $ to the end. This way the folder isn't
      visible if someone browses the shares on this server. For example,
      \\MyFileServer\MyPersonaShare$.

2. Set the share and local permissions to the group of View users as to reduce the number of people who have access to it. Set the permission for the share as shown in the following table:

User account	CIFS/SMB permissions
Creator Owner	**Full control – Subfolders and files only**
ViewUser group	**List folder / read data, Create folders / append data, and Read attributes – This folder only**
Everyone	No permissions
Local System	**Full control – This folder, subfolders and files**

The following screenshot shows the permission entry for share:

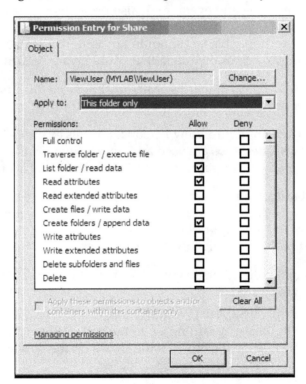

2. Copy the ViewPM.adm file to the AD server and add it to the Group Policies. Name it View Persona.

3. After the import we need to activate and specify the shared directory for View Persona GPO:

   1. Expand **Policies | Administrative Templates | Classic Administrative Templates | VMware View Agent Configuration | Persona Management | Roaming & Synchronization** as shown in the following screenshot:

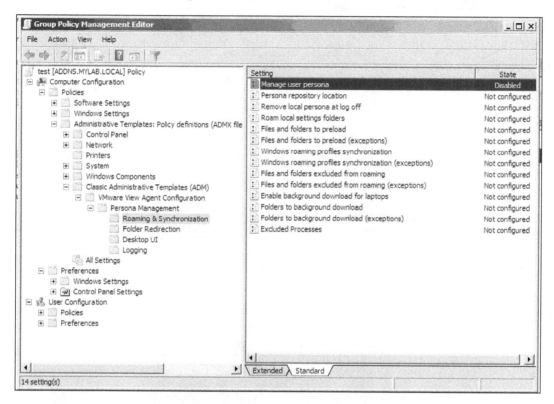

2. Double-click on **Manage user persona**.

3. In the new window, select **Enable** to enable View Persona.

4. Click on **Next Setting** (upper-right corner).

5. Now we are configuring the View Persona shared directory. To do so, select **Enable** and enter the path to the share. The override function is important if you have previously configured roaming profiles and would now like to use a different directory for Persona as shown in the following screenshot:

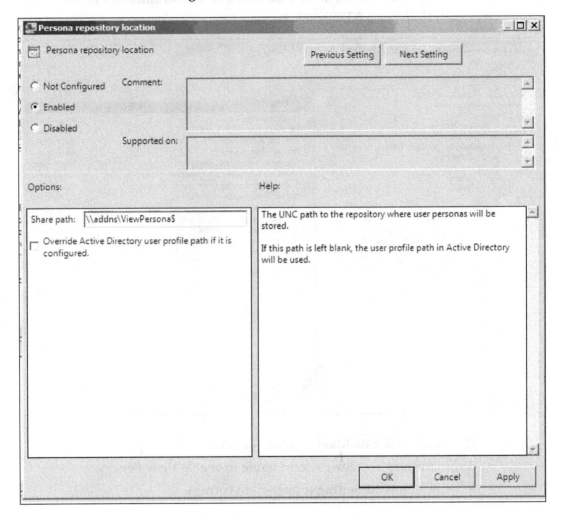

6. Browse through the rest of the setting and explore the other option. Then close the editor.

4. Now that we have added and configured the View AD template to the GPOs, we can assign it to the View desktop OU.

   1. Right-click on the View desktop OU and select **Link an existing GPO** as shown in the following screenshot:

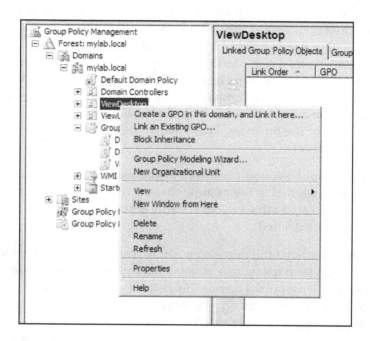

   2. Select the View Persona GPO from the menu.

Now, View Persona is set up and ready to go. Test by logging into a View desktop and then explore the share you created. It should now contain a subfolder with the username of the user you just logged on with.

Example setup

Let's take quick look at how this all works together. Let's imagine a middle-sized business where we have our office workers, our sales representatives and last but not least the IT guys.

In this scenario we could create a View environment that consists of only View Connection Servers because most workers are working in the office, however, let us assume we also want some workers to be able to work from home, so we add a security server that is configured to a proxy PCoIP over the Internet. This means we could use self-signed certs internally and trusted certs via the security server.

We should create three View desktop pools; one for the office workers, one for the sales reps, and one for the IT guys.

Let's start with the pool for the IT guys. That pool could be made up of persistent desktops that have all the needed software the admins need installed. Persona management isn't needed here as these VMs shouldn't contain any user data. All admin data is stored on a shared drive that is mapped to the desktops. We would allow USB forwarding (USB sticks and USB drives) as it comes in handy. Opening up the admin desktops for Local Mode and logging in via the Internet is a harder decision. A local admin desktop can be useful in **Disaster Recovery (DR)** situation; however, keeping it in sync is rather hard. Having the admin desktops available via the Internet allows the admins to work from home; however, it also exposes a great deal of the backbone of the business. I personally would disallow Local Mode and login via a security server.

The office workers could use non-persistent desktops with Persona management. USB forwarding isn't needed as we assume that the users are not allowed to connect them. This pool is also accessible via the security server so that users can work from home. Local Mode isn't needed.

The sales reps are mostly on the move so we may want them to be able to use Local Mode and even perhaps have access via the Internet. Local Mode should be configured to sync at least once a day as this helps the sales reps with backup. View Persona should be used too. Sales reps do have a need for USB devices, such as headsets (Skype) so we might want to allow these for them.

This little example should give you a general idea on how to incorporate all the little settings we have talked about.

Summary

In this chapter we looked at the client side of security and how simple modifications can increase security. A detailed look at the desktop pools settings as well as Local Mode showed us how to apply basic security to desktop pools. In the section about ADM templates we saw how to apply a great range of settings easily across a multitude of desktops.

In the next chapter we will dive into the challenges of backup and restore. We will discuss what to back up and how to restore. It also contains a look at patching a View environment.

5
Backup and Recovery

In this chapter, we will explore how to backup and recover a View environment.

We will also learn how to back up Views, which is a rather important security feature when things go wrong.

Backup and recovery

When we talk about backup, most people automatically think about the backup of the View desktops or the data within them. Only a very small set of View desktops need backup regularly, these are mostly persistent desktops for Admin or for special development purposes. In my opinion, the general View desktop doesn't need backup. All data that users touch should be on fileservers and the View desktop just a tool that can be redeployed on demand.

In regards of backup, each View environment splits up in three containers: VMware View Servers, vSphere, and infrastructure. Each of these components has its own backup requirements. But all these requirements need to be aligned as shown in the following diagram:

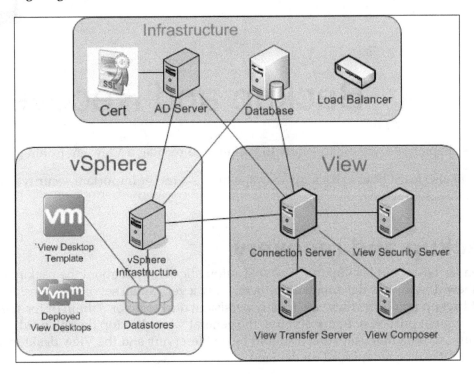

The vSphere environment

Let us start this section by diving into the backup at the root, the vSphere environment. The vSphere environment is the base on which VMware View runs. Not only do the View desktops run here but also the various View Servers. Backing up the vSphere environment is a book in itself; however I will shortly discuss the main components that require backup.

When we look at a vShpere 5.1 environment, we are looking at the following three main components: SSO, Inventory, and vCenter service. SSO and vCenter each require a database. Backing up the VM on which SSO and vCenter service are running is only good if you want a very fast recovery, however the most important piece to backup is the database where SSO and vCenter store their configuration.

You might want to backup the vSphere management VMs if you have added special configurations into the operation system, such as firewall rules or certificates. Most enterprises use tools from the storage or backup vendor to backup the complete datastores where all the VM's are stored. This makes the recovery of the base vSphere environment much easier and faster. But as said before the central pieces is the backup of the SSO and vCenter database. If you lose the database you will lose all configuration information of vSphere, which includes the configuration you set up for View (for example, users, folders, and many more). The important thing to understand here is that even if you rebuild the vCenter with the same folder or resource pool names, View will not be able to reconnect and use vCenter. The reason for this is that each object in vSphere has a **Managed object Reference (MoRef**) and View (as well as all other VMware products) uses the MoRef to talk to vCenter. The MoRef for each vSphere object is stored in the vCenter database.

As View and vSphere rely on each other, a backup of your View environment without a backup of the vSphere environment doesn't make any sense.

VMware View Servers

The View environment consists of the View Connection Servers, the View Security Servers, the View Composer (and its database) as well as some other components. The good news is that backup is a bit easier using the View Manager. The View Manager is able to extract all needed information from all the View servers and back them up centrally. However, the View Composer database should always be backed up regardless.

View Manager stores all information in its database. This database is an **Active Directory Application Mode (ADAM)** database, which is basically a LDAP based shared database. (see also `http://technet.microsoft.com/en-us/library/cc755705%28v=ws.10%29.aspx`) This database is located on the View Connection Servers. All entries in this database are replicated between all the View Connection Servers, which is another reason to create more than one View Connection Server.

Backing up all the View Connection Severs themselves is not really recommended. As all View Connection Servers share the same database, it is better to backup the configuration or one View Connection server and reinstall the others as replicas.

We will now run though a setup of the automated backup of the View ADAM database and the View Composer database. After this, we will look at the manual backup method.

To configure the automated backup of the View database follow these steps:

1. Log into the **View Administrator** console.

2. Expand **View Configuration** and click on **Servers**.

3. Right-click on one of the View Connection Servers and select **Edit**, as shown in the following screenshot:

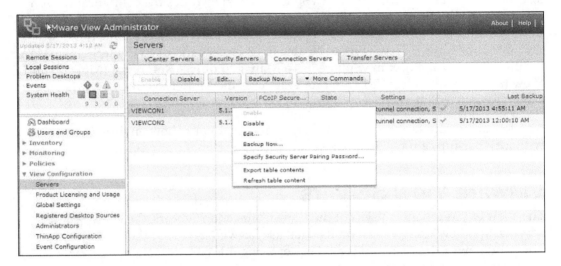

4. Click on the **Backup** tab, as shown in the following screenshot:

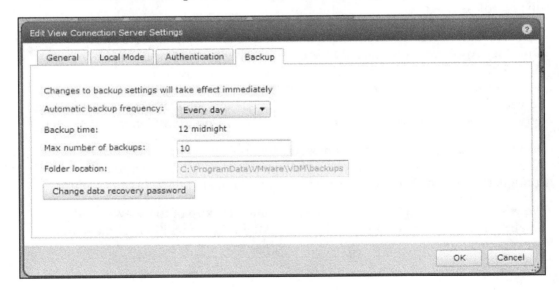

5. Now, you can specify the following **Backup** settings. You have to set these only once as all View Connection Servers replicate their information:

   ° **Automatic backup frequency**: How often should the backup run? You can configure these settings from **Every Hour** to **Never**.

   ° **Max number of backups**: Defines number of backup files that will be stored in the location. Old files will be deleted.

   ° **Folder location**: Defines where the backup files are stored, you may want to consider a network path here.

   ° **Change data recovery password**: You can set and change the recovery password. The password protects the backup files.

6. Click on **OK** to close the dialog.

To manually backup the View database follow these steps:

1. Log into the **View Administrator** console

2. Select **Pools** and select a View desktop pool.

3. Right-click on the pool, and for the new VMs, select **Disable provisioning**. Repeat this action for all pool to make sure no new data is written to the ADAM Database, refer to the following screenshot:

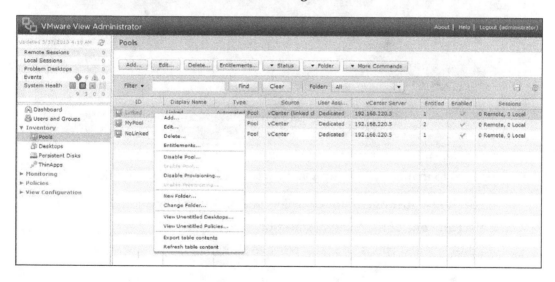

4. Repeat this for all View desktop pools. This will make sure that during the time of the back up no additional information will be written to the View database.

5. From here, there are two methods that can be used, either the manual method that allows for scripting the backup or the View Administrator console initiated version.

Let us see how to manually back up via DOS console.

1. The export of the ADAM database is done via the export tool that is installed on the View Connections Server:

   `C:\Program Files\VMware\VMware View\Server\tools\bin\ vdmexport.exe`

2. Run the `vdmexport.exe` command with the `-f` key to specify a location:

   vdmexport -f c:\tmp\vdmconfig.ldf

   The following screenshot shows how to do this:

```
Administrator: C:\Windows\system32\cmd.exe                              _ □ ×
C:\Users\administrator.MYLAB>cd c:\

c:\>cd "Program Files\VMware\VMware View\Server\tools\bin"

c:\Program Files\VMware\VMware View\Server\tools\bin>vdmexport -f c:\tmp\vdmconf
ig.ldf

c:\Program Files\VMware\VMware View\Server\tools\bin>dir  c:\tmp
 Volume in drive C has no label.
 Volume Serial Number is 98A6-4BE1

 Directory of c:\tmp

05/17/2013  04:43 AM    <DIR>          .
05/17/2013  04:43 AM    <DIR>          ..
05/17/2013  04:43 AM         4,091,614 vdmconfig.ldf
               1 File(s)      4,091,614 bytes
               2 Dir(s)  31,962,808,320 bytes free

c:\Program Files\VMware\VMware View\Server\tools\bin>
```

Let us see how to manually back up via the View Administrator console

1. In the **View Administrator** console, click on **Inventory** and select **Servers**.

2. Select any one of the View Connection Server.

3. Right-click and choose **Backup Now** as shown in the following screenshot:

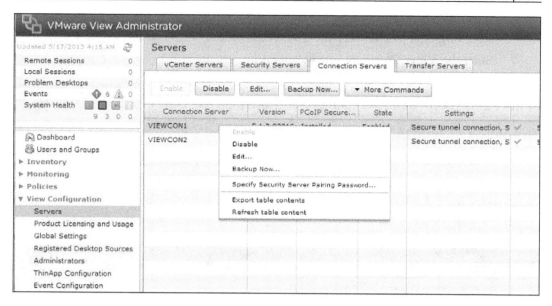

To manually backup the View Composer database follow these steps:

1. Log in to the View Administrator console.
2. Select **Pools** and select a View desktop pool.
3. Right-click on the **Pool** and for new VMs, select **Disable provisioning**.
4. Log in to the VM where the View Composer is installed.
5. Stop the View Composer service. This will stop all further provisioning request for creating linked clones, which would change data in the View Composer database as shown in the following screenshot:

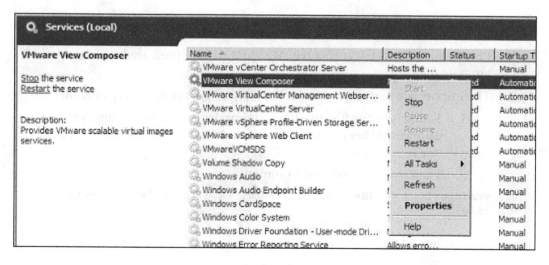

6. After the Composer service is stopped the Composer database can be backed up using best practice for the given database.

7. Start the View Composer service again.

After backup the next important thing is restore. We will now walk through a restore of the View ADAM database configuration and then the View Composer Database.

To restore a View ADAM Database follow these steps:

1. If you have multiple View Connection Servers, the best way is to stop them and delete them. You will later have to reinstall them as replica servers.

2. Log in to the **View Connection Server**.

3. Stop the View Connection Server service as shown in the following screenshot:

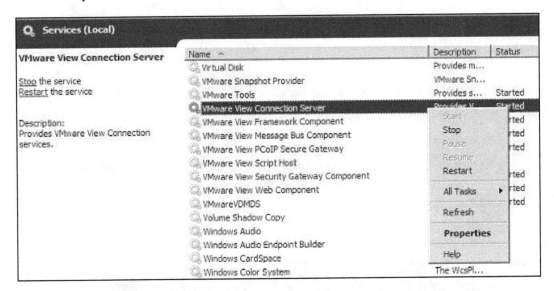

4. Locate the export/backup of the ADAM database (you are looking for an .ldf file).

5. The import is a two-step process. First, we will have to decrypt the file.

    1. To decrypt the file, use the vdmimport tool locate on any View Connection Server in C:\Program Files\VMware\VMware View\ Server\tools\bin.

    2. Then use the following command:

```
vdmimport -d -p [Recovery password] -f [.ldf file] > [decrypted file]
```

6. The second step is to import the decrypted file, again using the vdmimport tool. Run the following command:

```
vdmimport -f  [decrypted file]
```

The following screenshot shows how to do this:

7. The View ADAM database is now updated.

8. Start the View Connection service.

9. Reinstall all other View Connection Server as replica servers.

To restore a View Composer database follow these steps:

1. Log into the VM where the View Composer is installed.

2. Stop the **View Composer** service.

3. Restore the View Composer database using best practice of the database vendor.

4. Start the **View Composer** service.

Basic infrastructure

Next to the VMware vSphere environment, the common Infrastructure environment is rather important in the backup process.

The clearest target for backup is the database server that contains the vSphere, View Composer database, and the View Connection server event database. How to back up these databases is up to the best practice of the database vendor. However these databases should be backed up regularly. Restoring these databases requires that the system that uses them is shut down.

The other important to thing about backup is the **Active Directory** (**AD**) part. We will leave the best methods of backing up and restoring AD to best practice of Microsoft. You might already know why AD is such an important thing. In the preparation to install View, you created certain **Organization Units** (**OUs**) and users with special rights (review *VMware Installation Guide*). In addition to that we used AD in the last chapter to configure security rules for client connections, USB access, and so on. If your AD is also a CA for your SSL Certs, then it even becomes more important to backup your AD. Restoring you AD is again left to best-practice of Microsoft. When AD is restored, we just can resume operations.

With respect to AD, it is a good idea when creating new GPO rules to create a separate backup for these rules. This is how you create a backup of an GPO:

1. Login to your AD server.

2. Open the **Group Policy Management** by navigating to **Start | Administrative Tools | Group Policy Management**, as shown in the following screenshot:

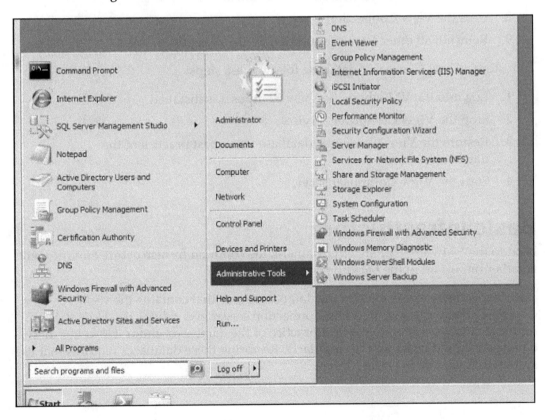

3. Expand your domain and find the **Group Policy Object (GPO)**.

4. Find the GPO you configured and right-click on it as shown in the following screenshot:

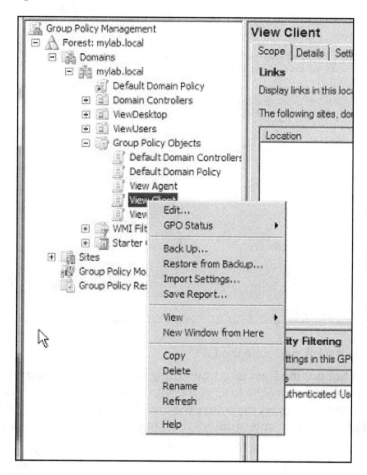

5. Select **Back Up ...** from the right-click menu.

6. Select a location to store the backup, as shown in the following screenshot:

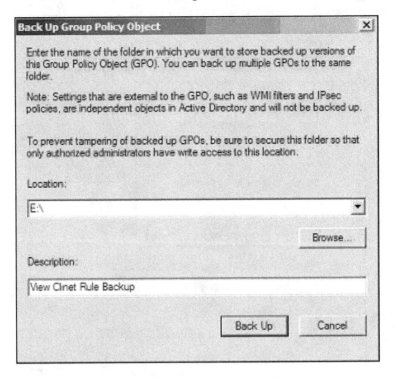

7. Click on **Back Up** to save the GPO.

8. The last but not the least important thing here is the load balancer that is setup for balancing the load of the View Connection or View Security Servers. Depending on the setup, the load balancer might have SSL Certificate installed or special configurations, backing these settings up once is enough.

Desktop pools and linked cloning

Backup becomes much more complicated when we take a look at already provisioned View desktop. There are basically two types of desktop pools: full provisioned VM and linked clone pools. The following screenshot shows the exact structure:

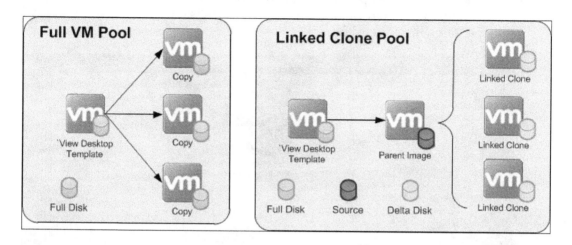

When a View desktop is provisioned as a full VM Pool, the View template VM is cloned and the View client connects to the View Agent installed on the VM. If the View desktop template is missing, the View VMs will still be working fine, however no new View desktops can be provisioned. When a linked View desktop pool is provisioned and the View desktop template is missing, new desktops can be provisioned because the linked clone parent still exists and additional linked clones can be provisioned. However it's better to go back and rectify this situation as soon as possible. That is done by recomposing a linked clone pool.

Follow these instructions to recompose a linked clone environment:

1. Log into the **View Administrator** console.

2. Expend **Inventory** and select **Pools**.

3. By disabling the pool provisioning, you make sure that while the reconfigure is running no new desktops are provisioned, as shown in the following screenshot:

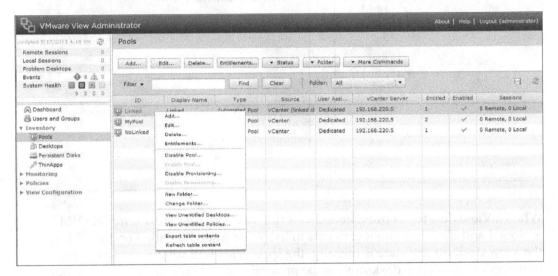

4. Double-click on the desktop pool you want to recompose.

5. Click on **View Composer** and select **Recompose** all desktops in the Pool, as shown in the following screenshot:

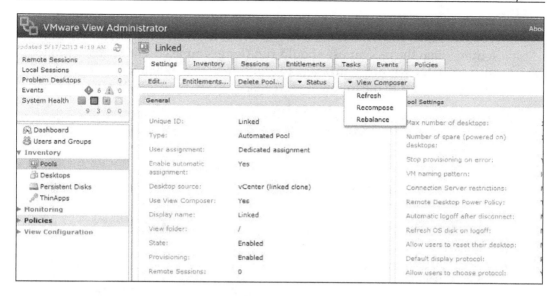

6. Choose the new image (the recovered one and an appropriate snapshot) and make sure to tick the **Change the default image for new desktops** option, as shown in the following screenshot:

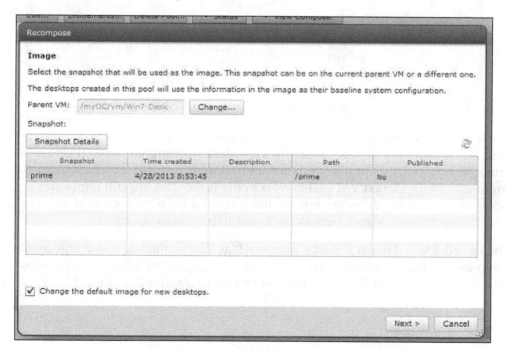

7. While users are logged in, desktops cannot be recomposed. To rectify this you can either force the users to log off, wait until they log off, or schedule a time when the recompose should run (for example, at night). You should also consider sending a message to all users in this pool telling them what is going on. Refer to the following screenshot to see how it is done:

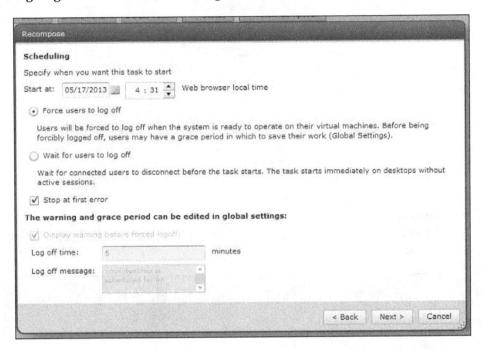

8. Finish the wizard implementation. The desktop will now recompose.

If linked clones or the parent image has gone missing there is nothing that can be done, but to redeploy the pool from the View desktop template. Linked clones cannot be restored, except if a *full* datastore backup is restored which contains the parent and all the cloned VM's. This works only if the VMs are still registered in vSphere, so when the datastore returns the VM's still have the correct MoRef for View Composer and View Connection Server to be able to use them.

When a full VM is deleted it can be recovered, as long as the VM is still registered in vSphere. If this is not the case the MoRef has changed. The VM will still run but VMware View Connection Server will not be able to connect the VM to a View Client.

The important lesson from this section is to make sure that important data is not stored on the View desktops. Using remote profiles and shares to store the user data will improve the security and backup of this data.

Documenting – the ultimate backup

One of the best backup methods is to document all settings and changes in a document. Actually there should be several documents, such as design, configuration, and build documents.

A design document would record all design decisions made and explain why they were made. This is an important document that will help to redesign, expand, and update a View installation. A design document is not changed often, as it shows basic layout of the solution and should only be updated if the layout changes.

A configuration document records all configuration settings for each of the components installed. Typically there would be one configuration documents for the View Connection Servers, one for the AD domains, and one for the DMZ. Each of these documents show all settings and should be updated when these settings are changed.

A build document contains detailed instructions on how to install certain software. These documents change only between versions of the software. The idea of these documents is to record all special installations steps that have to be done in a given environment.

The basic principle of documentation is that it is the last line of defense and a source of information. Information is important. I cannot count the amount of projects that were impacted because certain software installation had no documentation that explained what they interacted with, how they were configured and installed. Not having this information leads to delays or worse to the cancelation of projects.

Backup timing

Backup is all about timing. Creating a backup consumes space and also documentation. Should you need to restore, you will need to know which backup to restore from. This requires the knowledge of what backup was taken when and from what. Let's shed some light on some of these.

Let's start with something easy like the View desktop template. As discussed earlier, the View desktop template is the source of all View desktop pools. The View desktop template is an inactive VM that sits on the vSphere environment. Backup is only required if the template changes. So a once off backup is enough. However, it is also a good idea to document the settings of the View desktop pools.

The same goes for the AD GPO's and the certificates; a backup/export of them is a good idea when they change.

Things that need a more regularly backup are View databases as well as the settings of the View and the vSphere environment.

The other aspect of timing is to understand how fast you need to restore. All these things should normally be covered in the design document. However let's review some ideas on this topic. Typical questions you should ask yourself are:

- How long can your business function without desktops?
- Which desktops need to be recovered first, for example, administrative desktops?
- If there are different View environments (for example, DMZ) are they all critical to be recovered at the same time?
- What pre-requisites must be recovered before a given View environment or pool can be recovered (for example, data sources)?
- When is a good time for backup? What time are no provisioning or destroy actions running on the View environment?
- Is the backup I'm running restorable? And how long do certain restore scenarios take?

The last question is the most important question. It is imperative to test the restore of your environment. This will provide you with a lot of benefits such as: the actual recovery timing, training on how to do it, the accuracy of the restore documentation, and last but not the least does your current backup regiment fulfills your requirements.

Patching the View environment

One of the many things you should do on a regular basis is patching, which should include the patching of the View servers and the View desktops.

This is not only done for View updates but more importantly for Windows updates to the server and to the desktop templates. To patch a View server with View updates, I highly recommend following the instructions that come with the View update (the release notes).

View server

To patch the View servers it is best if you have multiple View servers of any flavor, so you can patch the whole environment without interruption to the clients. It is however important to think back to the basics. When patching a View Connection Server that is the target of a View Security Server it makes sense to follow these steps:

1. Log onto the View Connection Server.
2. Stop the View Connection service.
3. Patch the View Connection Server with Windows updates.
4. Log onto the View Security Server associated with this View Connection Server.
5. Stop the View Security service.
6. Patch the View Security Server with Windows updates.
7. Start the View Connection service.
8. Start the View Security service.

View desktops

The patching of View desktop is a bit different. Patching a linked clone View desktop pool it is rather easy, you can use the recompose function, as we did earlier when we talked about restoring a desktop pool while, if you are patching a full clone pool, you will have to roll out new clones

The first basic steps are the same for linked and non-linked desktop pools:

1. Log in to the **View Administrator** console.
2. Select **Pools** and select a View desktop pool.
3. Right-click on the pool and for new VMs, select **Disable provisioning**. This step will insure that no new cloning activities are started and that we can modify the source.
4. Log in to vSphere.
5. Find your View desktop template.
6. If you are using multiple snapshots in the same VM, you need to select the one you want to alter.
7. Power-on the View desktop template.
8. Connect to the View desktop template and update the image as required.
9. Shut down the View desktop template.

At this stage we need to split off into linked and non-linked desktop pools.

For linked clone pools, follow these instructions:

1. Log into the **View Administrator** console.
2. Select **Pools** and select a View desktop pool.
3. Double-click on the pool you want to recompose.
4. Choose recompose all desktops in the pool.
5. Click on **View Composer** and select **Recompose**.
6. Finish the wizard implementation. The desktop will now recompose.

For non-linked clone, follow these instructions:

1. Log into the **View Administrator** console.
2. Select **Pools** and select a View desktop pool.
3. Right-click and select refresh.

Desktops with local mode must be be checked in when recomposed. Alternatively you can roll back the local View desktop to force the new image onto the client.

Summary

This concludes our overview of backup and restore of a View environment. We looked at the vSphere backups and talked about the View environment backups and how interconnected they are. We discussed what to backup when and the important points of what really needs backup. Last but not the least, we also took a good look at restore operations, both automated and manually.

The patching of an View environment was also discussed. We talked about how to apply patching and what systems will be impacted, making it easier to asses the impact of patching on a productive environment.

Index

Thank you for buying
VMware View Security Essentials

About Packt Publishing

Packt, pronounced 'packed', published its first book "Mastering phpMyAdmin for Effective MySQL Management" in April 2004 and subsequently continued to specialize in publishing highly focused books on specific technologies and solutions.

Our books and publications share the experiences of your fellow IT professionals in adapting and customizing today's systems, applications, and frameworks. Our solution based books give you the knowledge and power to customize the software and technologies you're using to get the job done. Packt books are more specific and less general than the IT books you have seen in the past. Our unique business model allows us to bring you more focused information, giving you more of what you need to know, and less of what you don't.

Packt is a modern, yet unique publishing company, which focuses on producing quality, cutting-edge books for communities of developers, administrators, and newbies alike. For more information, please visit our website: www.packtpub.com.

About Packt Enterprise

In 2010, Packt launched two new brands, Packt Enterprise and Packt Open Source, in order to continue its focus on specialization. This book is part of the Packt Enterprise brand, home to books published on enterprise software – software created by major vendors, including (but not limited to) IBM, Microsoft and Oracle, often for use in other corporations. Its titles will offer information relevant to a range of users of this software, including administrators, developers, architects, and end users.

Writing for Packt

We welcome all inquiries from people who are interested in authoring. Book proposals should be sent to author@packtpub.com. If your book idea is still at an early stage and you would like to discuss it first before writing a formal book proposal, contact us; one of our commissioning editors will get in touch with you.

We're not just looking for published authors; if you have strong technical skills but no writing experience, our experienced editors can help you develop a writing career, or simply get some additional reward for your expertise.

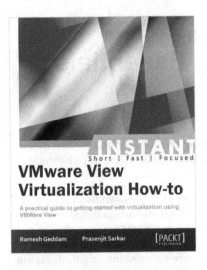

Instant VMware View Virtualization How-to

ISBN: 978-1-84968-916-8   Paperback: 76 pages

A practical guide to getting started with virtualization using VMWare View

1. Learn something new in an Instant! A short, fast, focused guide delivering immediate results

2. Implement virtualization on Windows 8

3. Learn details that are not available in the VDI documentation of VMware View

4. Learn about the advanced features of VMWare View 5.x

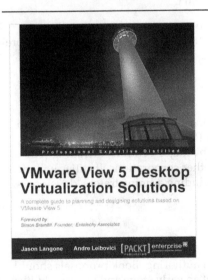

VMware View 5 Desktop Virtualization Solutions

ISBN: 978-1-84968-112-4   Paperback: 288 pages

A complete guide to planning and designing solutions based on VMware View 5

1. Written by VMware experts Jason Langone and Andre Leibovici, this book is a complete guide to planning and designing a solution based on VMware View 5

2. Secure your Visual Desktop Infrastructure (VDI) by having firewalls, antivirus, virtual enclaves, USB redirection and filtering and smart card authentication

3. Analyze the strategies and techniques used to migrate a user population from a physical desktop environment to a virtual desktop solution

Please check **www.PacktPub.com** for information on our titles

VMware vSphere 5.1
Cookbook

Over 130 task-oriented recipes to install, configure, and manage
various vSphere 5.1 components

Abhilash GB

VMware vSphere 5.1 Cookbook

ISBN: 978-1-84968-402-6   Paperback: 466 pages

Over 130 task-oriented recipes to install, configure,
and manage various vSphere 5.1 components

1. Install and configure vSphere 5.1 core
   components

2. Learn important aspects of vSphere such as
   administration, security, and performance

3. Configure vSphere Management
   Assistant(VMA) to run commands/scripts
   without the need to authenticate every attempt

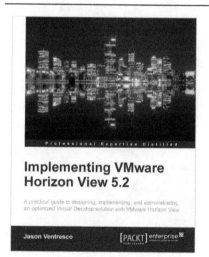

Implementing VMware
Horizon View 5.2

A practical guide to designing, implementing, and administrating
an optimized Virtual Desktop solution with VMware Horizon View

Jason Ventresco

Implementing VMware Horizon View 5.2

ISBN: 978-1-84968-796-6   Paperback: 390 pages

A practical guide to designing, implementing, and
administrating an optimized Virtual Desktop solution
with VMware Horizon View

1. Detailed description of the deployment
   and administration of the VMware Horizon
   View suite

2. Learn how to determine the resources your
   virtual desktops will require

3. Design your desktop solution to avoid potential
   problems, and ensure minimal loss of time in
   the later stages

Please check **www.PacktPub.com** for information on our titles